BROKEN MOMENTS

From Shattered to Masterpiece

COMPILED AND EDITED BY
YVONNE LEHMAN

Royalties for this book are donated to Samaritan's Purse.

BROKEN MOMENTS: FROM SHATTERED TO MASTERPIECE

ISBN-13: 978-1-60495-075-5

From Samaritan's Purse

We so appreciate your donating all royalties from the sale of the books *Divine Moments, Christmas Moments, Spoken Moments, Precious Precocious Moments, More Christmas Moments, Stupid Moments, Additional Christmas Moments, Loving Moments, Merry Christmas Moments, Coolinary Moments, Moments with Billy Graham, Personal Titanic Moments, Remembering Christmas, Romantic Moments, Pandemic Moments, Christmas Stories,* and now *Broken Moments* to Samaritan's Purse.

What a blessing that you would think of us! Thank you for your willingness to bless others and bring glory to God through your literary talents. Grace and peace to you.

Their Mission Statement:

Samaritan's Purse is a nondenominational evangelical Christian organization providing spiritual and physical aid to hurting people around the world.

Since 1970, Samaritan's Purse has helped victims of war, poverty, natural disasters, disease, and famine with the purpose of sharing God's love through his son, Jesus Christ.

Go and do likewise
Luke 10:37

You can learn more by visiting their website at
samaritanspurse.org

Foreword

The cover image is an example of *Kintsugi* (golden repair), the Japanese technique of repairing broken pottery with a special lacquer mixed with powdered gold.

Kintsugi treats breakage and repair as part of the history of an object, rather than something to disguise. Because both the lacquer and gold are expensive, mending the vessel adds beauty and value.

With this technique, it is possible to create works of art that are always different, each with its own story and beauty as a result of the unique cracks and breaks formed when the object was damaged — similar to the wounds that leave different marks on each of us.

Kintsugi restorations are so obvious that they can be considered nothing less than celebrations. Those now precious scars have become seams of gold, the formerly broken places highlighted in ways that bring greater beauty than would be possible if not for having broken.

It's a perfect representation of the way God heals His people! When we allow Christ to heal our brokenness, we become His masterpieces, truly different works of art, each with our own story and beauty.

It is also a powerful visual reminder to us that it does not matter if anyone — including ourselves — thinks we are damaged beyond repair. When we allow Christ to mend the broken pieces of our lives, we become vessels of astounding strength and beauty.

On the following pages you'll find stories of various types of brokenness — from objects to people — and how, in each instance, that brokenness was redeemed.

Table of Contents

1

Out of My Brokenness

Norma C. Mezoe

Time seemed to stand still as I paced the floor. Blackness enveloped me. Earlier that night my husband had sat across the table from me, his eyes averted. Finally he said he must leave, that he had some thinking to do. I knew something was desperately wrong but could only wonder about the extent of the problem.

The next morning when I asked the reason for his leaving the night before, he threw a bombshell at me. It touched every part of my being and left me shattered. He explained that he was leaving me because he had fallen in love with a young mother who attended the church he was pastoring.

My world crumbled; and I seemed to be standing in the midst of an earthquake.

We had survived so many crises together — financial, family problems, major surgeries. How could my husband walk away from all the memories of things we had experienced together?

When I told one of our daughters that her father had chosen another woman, she simply stared at me and replied, "Dad?" That one word spoke volumes. The tragedy that could never happen to our family had happened. Our three children were grown, but like young children in broken homes, they suffered a gamut of emotions, beginning with shock and disbelief.

During the next weeks, when I worshipped in our church and listened as a supply minister stood in the pulpit where my husband had stood, my eyes filled with tears. Watching a couple as they looked lovingly at one another reinforced the fact that I was now alone.

But an ever-present God and loving friends carried me through the aftershock. I was filled with an incredible peace and joy. Some thought I needed to release my emotions. Yet God's hands seemed to be drying my eyes before the tears had an opportunity to form.

I wondered how I would support myself. I had never been employed outside our home. I had enjoyed being a wife and mother to our three children for twenty-seven years. Now I was faced with the necessity of seeking employment. I asked myself, "What will I do? Where will I turn?" I was living out in the country without transportation. If I did find employment, how would I get to work? Through all of these questions and many others, God was quietly and wondrously working. His plans for my life as a single woman were slowly evolving.

One day a friend from our former church came to visit with news about a possible job. Her daughter was secretary at an organization that was seeking telephone recruiters for a one-month period at minimum pay. My friend asked if I would be interested.

"Vee," I replied, "I believe God has sent you to tell me this. I would like to apply for the position." I applied for and was given the job. The office was located thirty-five miles from the parsonage where I was living at the time. I was still without transportation. Then, the day before I began my temporary work, I was given a car, complete with license plate and paid insurance.

It was quite an experience rising early in the morning and driving those thirty-five miles to a large city. I spent my driving time singing praises to God — my heavenly Father and my Friend — who loved me so much.

Day after day I sat at a telephone, recruiting workers. At times the work was frustrating and tiring, but it was a stimulating experience. I was on my own, yet I was never alone, for God's presence surrounded me; His Spirit was in me and around me. I seemed to feel His gentle touch.

I needed to talk during those days and weeks after my husband left. So many emotions were bottled up inside me, talking was my way of releasing frustrations. One dear friend phoned every evening after I returned from work. She patiently listened as I asked questions and related unending details of my new job.

One and a half weeks after I began work as a recruiter, the secretary resigned her position. She asked if I would be interested in applying for the job. That night I toiled over a resume, and prepared for an interview with the supervisor the next morning. Instead of listing places of employment, I wrote of the experiences and skills I had gathered throughout my years of homemaking and serving as a minister's wife. The next morning I prayed silently as I answered the supervisor's questions. I was hired as a district secretary of the nationwide organization.

One of my responsibilities is to counsel people who have heartbreaking problems. God is using my brokenness to serve not only Himself, but also others.

More than four years have passed since that long, lonely time when I felt that my entire life was over. I thought I had arrived at my road's end. In reality, it was not the end but a turn that brought me to a deeper commitment to God and His leading. From the beginning I claimed Romans 8:28: *We know that in all things God works for the good of those who love him, who have been called according to his purpose.*

I clung to this promise during the months that followed. There were moments I didn't understand how God could possibly bring good from the heartache I was experiencing. Now, as I look back over the past four years, I can see many ways in which God fulfilled and continues to fulfill the promise of Romans 8:28 in my life.

God has brought people struggling with heartaches my way, and I have had the opportunity to offer encouragement. To them I can offer a cup of cool water in Christ's name.

God continues to fulfill His promise to bring good out of bad, and through His loving grace I have discovered new strengths in myself.

I know that God's will is that marriage be a lifetime commitment. But when that option is closed, there is yet hope. In God's love I can still be a vital Christian, living a full life and sharing His love with others who need encouragement. God does give victory to overcome discouragement and depression and He does give meaning to life. I know this is true because He has brought blessings out of my brokenness.

2

In Need of Rescue

Krista Lynn Campbell

Thump, thump, thump forced an emergency pullover. In front of me rose a massive mound. As the moon illuminated the mountain, foul odors confirmed my location. I was stranded at the county landfill with a flat tire.

Earlier, when the strange yellow light had appeared on my dashboard, I had ignored it for several miles. Probably nothing, I assumed. But a gas station stop revealed otherwise. The manual buried in the glove compartment identified the mysterious warning symbol: Low Tire Pressure Indicator.

I exited the car and viewed the culprit — a low rear tire.

No problem. I had this. A few pumps of air inflated the tire, boosted my resolve, and I continued home. Soon, the light blinked on again. Four gas stations, a can of Fix-A-Flat, and many tears later, I maneuvered my wounded confidence and vehicle into the landfill's parking lot.

I'd lost the battle. An attempt to limp home on three good tires and one compromised piece of rubber had landed me with smelly garbage. How appropriate, I thought. My rotten mood matched the rancid surroundings.

I raised the white flag, called roadside assistance, and emptied a box of tissues. A forty-five minute wait afforded me time to contemplate my circumstances alone in the dark.

- Do I ignore God's warning signs like my car's indicator lights: Do not speak those words! Do not judge another! Do not click on that site!

- Do I barrel through life with an "I've got this" attitude and then suffer the consequences: a busted tire and a broken life?
- Do I pursue quick fixes: like my futile attempts to pump air into a leaking tire?

Yes, yes, and yes.

Limping around on a flat tire leaves me exhausted and frustrated.

With open arms, my Heavenly Father invites me to release and rest. Matthew 11:28 tells us, *Come to me, all you who are weary and burdened, and I will give you rest.*

Oh, I was weary and burdened. I needed rest and a shower. Kneeling on rough pavement with a filthy tire left me dirty and distressed.

I needed rescue — someone to save me and help me get home, safe and sound.

The words from Psalm 121:1-3 came to mind: *I lift up my eyes to the mountains – where does my help come from? My help comes from the Lord, the Maker of heaven and earth. He will not let your foot slip – he who watches over you will not slumber."*

A pair of bright headlights broke through the darkness as the service truck approached. No longer alone, I experienced relief and comfort in my rescuer's company. With smooth efficiency the flat tire was replaced, hope (and sanity) restored.

I offered a silent prayer of thanksgiving.

A warm shower and soft bed welcomed me home. Time to rest under the watchful eye of my true Rescuer.

In the garbage pit of life's flat tires, I feel alone, unworthy of redemption, and broken beyond repair. But my never-sleeping Rescuer sees me busted, defeated, and deflated just like the tire. God hears my cry and comes to the rescue. He kneels beside my brokenness, gathers me in His arms, and whispers, "I've got this. Rest in Me."

As He tells us in Isaiah 46:4: *Even to your old age and gray hairs I am he, I am he who will sustain you. I have made you and I will carry you; I will sustain you and I will rescue you.*

3

God, You Promised

Helen L. Hoover

What happened here, God? You promised. Why didn't you answer my prayer? Are any of Your promises true? How can I trust You with other areas of my life?" Railing at God didn't help my frustration that day, because God didn't answer.

Two months earlier, Gary, my twenty-three year old son, had shot himself. Over the previous two years a divorce, loss of his job, challenges in seeing his young daughter, and the break-up with a girlfriend had combined to lead to hopelessness and then depression for my talented, loving son. He had given up on church, God, and finally life.

A year before his death, I had claimed for him the scripture Jeremiah 31:16-17: *This is what the LORD says: "Restrain your voice from weeping and your eyes from tears, for your work will be rewarded," declares the LORD. "They will return from the land of the enemy. So there is hope for your future," declares the LORD. "Your children will return to their own land.*

I had heard various Christian sources recommend claiming God's promises for ourselves and our family members. This scripture seemed appropriate for Gary, so I had dutifully prayed and asked God to fulfill this in Gary's life. I thought the phrase "your work will be rewarded" applied to the Godly ways and principles I had taught him while he grew up. As a youngster Gary had accepted Christ as his Savior, so returning "to their own land" would entail returning to church and trusting God with his life. I had been looking forward to Gary coming back to his Christian roots and then serving God again.

When I finally began to surface from my grief and numbness after Gary's death, I remembered the Scripture promise I had claimed for my hurting child. I was troubled that it didn't seem to have "worked." I began to question God and His promises. If this scripture didn't work for Gary, would trusting God to fulfill any Scripture work? I still believed in God's love and a future in heaven, but maybe claiming Scripture promises was foolish. Why did God issue the promises if they weren't true?

The days turned into weeks as I walked in a daze through the various stages of grief. I still had no answer concerning the scripture for Gary or the truth of claiming scriptures for various situations. My trust in God was broken and I didn't know what to do about it. I backed off of reading my Bible and praying, even while faithfully attending church. Inside I was in turmoil. What was the truth about God's promises?

One day, about six months later, while missing my son and thinking about the scripture, I knew God told me in my heart, "He did return."

"How could that be, Lord?" Then I knew. Gary was with God. Gary had returned to his final destination.

Sobbing, I thanked God for taking Gary home, even though it wasn't as I had envisioned. I then could say, "You are faithful to Your promises, God."

Gradually I came back to trusting God for every area of my life and I now have scriptures I claim for other family members. I realize, though, I can't box God in with the way I think situations should turn out. He knows the big picture and I only see a tiny portion. His faithfulness to His promises doesn't depend upon me understanding or determining how He carries them out.

Your kingdom is an everlasting kingdom, and your dominion endures through all generations. The LORD is faithful to all his promises and loving toward all he has made.
Psalm 145:13

4

Choose Joy

Diana C. Derringer

Rejoice in the Lord always.
Philippians 4:4

Stage III anaplastic astrocytoma, a malignant brain tumor, too near speech and memory centers to remove surgically."

Those words, addressing my husband's physical symptoms, began a life-changing journey that continues today. In the course of this journey we've felt God's presence, peace, and joy in ways previously unknown.

Although initial tests indicated probable non-malignancy, the biopsy revealed an aggressive malignant mass. After receiving that gut-wrenching news, we faced the daunting task of calling friends and family and addressing their subsequent concerns.

Like robots, we automatically did what had to be done. We made appointments for treatments, filled prescriptions, completed insurance forms, and trekked the mountain of other health-related chores. We shed a few tears, prayed, and tried to sort through the bombardment of feelings. With an average life expectancy of three to five years for this diagnosis, the stages of grief took on a whole new meaning.

Sometimes we felt like yo-yos with an unknown force controlling the string. A false negative test days before initial treatment gave a brief reprieve, only to be shot down when a follow-up evaluation confirmed the grimmer report.

Through all the ups and downs we've learned several valuable life lessons. One stands out from them all: Although we have no control over a number of life's circumstances, the reaction remains ours to make.

In day-to-day life we can see faults in others and withdraw from relationships, or we can be grateful others overlook our bad habits, and do the same for them. We can grumble about our jobs and co-workers or be thankful for the opportunity to earn a steady income. We can criticize neighbors or appreciate their willingness to help in time of need. We can focus on material possessions we don't have or recall that we have sufficient provisions for our needs. We can despair when illness and age make daily life more difficult, or we can face new challenges with determination and make the most of our abilities.

We all face the questions. Do we desire a life of defeat and gloom or one of victory and joy? Will we worry over every detail of life or hand each one to our loving Lord who remains with us through all life's peaks and valleys? Will we claim Jesus' promises or agonize over every bump in the road?

In Matthew 6:27 Jesus tells us worry can't add a day to our lives. I firmly believe it not only can't add a day but also shortens our days and deprives us of countless blessings during both our best and hardest times.

We've now enjoyed more than nine years of remission (thirteen years plus from initial diagnosis). Of course, we have no guarantee for what the future holds. Who does? Yet, even on our worst days, we rest in the knowledge of God's love and care.

Regardless of our circumstances or the direction this journey takes, we've made our choice. We trade our worries for worship and our sorrow for service.

We choose joy!

5

But God . . .

Ken Carver

K enneth, we need you down here. We need you now!"
But God . . .

I was working at my retirement job and trying to expand my freelance writing business, all the while trying to see after my aged parents who lived two hundred twenty-five miles away. I was their only child.

The "Kenneth, we need you now . . ." phone call landed atop dozens of others that had piled up over the past year. Mom was eighty-nine, Dad ninety-three. Physically and mentally they were spiraling downward at a steadily increasing rate.

"Mom, Dad, if you don't decide which assisted living facility you prefer, when the crisis comes — and it *will* come — I'll have to decide for you." We'd had that conversation many times over several years. They'd never made a decision, and now the crisis was here.

I arranged with my retirement-job employer to be off for an indefinite time period, told my wife I'd be back ASAP — whenever that might be — and left the next day, praying again for God to give me wisdom, discernment and common sense to make good decisions. En route I spoke with their primary care doctor. "You've got to move them, Mr. Carver," he said. "Now."

"Roger, Wilco," I said in military parlance. "I understand and will comply."

During the next thirty days, Dad was admitted to a hospital for psychiatric evaluation, and I made arrangements for him and Mom in an assisted living facility near my home. Mom was shocked that the crisis had really come and that I had made good on my promise to take charge. No options for them remained on the table.

During those thirty days I had to do something else. I had to back out of some magazine writing assignments. I called my editor, who seemed to understand my plight, and agreed to give the assignments to someone else. I was to call him after things calmed down and my life was back to normal.

It didn't happen. My writing momentum was broken.

Getting my parents settled into their new home was just the beginning of the demands I faced. Those demands broke the cycle of assignments I was enjoying. Worse, they broke my desire to write. I had a new mission, unwanted but unavoidable.

I had to find new doctors. That's doctors — plural. Old folks require numerous doctors.

Their house had to be emptied. An estate sale took care of most of that. (Did you know that someone will buy almost anything at an estate sale?) Then it had to be cleaned and sold in a down-market.

Mom and Dad were dead and buried within a year, within seven weeks of each other.

My grief was really a sense of joy in many ways. I didn't rejoice that they were gone, but I rejoiced that they were unburdened from all the physical, mental and emotional baggage they had carried for so long. They were with Jesus in heaven, of that I was confident. Their verbal testimonies and lifestyles gave evidence of their salvation.

So now it was time to get back into writing. Right?

Not really. Somehow the fire was gone. I didn't want it to be, but it was. I couldn't find it. The ashes were cold.

But God . . .

Don't you love those two little words?

Even though God didn't reignite my desire to write — not at that point anyway — He gave me the desire to help others with their writing.

So I became a freelance editor. Other people I knew were trying their hands at the writing craft and asked me to look over their work.

Initially, they focused on the free part of freelance, but I saw that God was giving me a way to replace a little of my previous writing income. Remarkably, they understood.

Today, that editing avenue continues to be a blessing to me. But God — there it is again — seems to be rekindling my desire to write, for Him, for myself.

Proverbs 3:5-6 (NLT) tells us, *Trust the LORD with all your heart; do not depend on your own understanding. Seek his will in all you do, and he will show you which path to take.*

This story is the first thing I've *wanted* to write for publication in almost ten years. God willing, it won't be the last.

There's no brokenness this time.

God simply continues to direct my path.

6

Sticks and Stones

Nanette Thorsen-Snipes

I paused, the Coke can in my hand still midair. Which cup did she want me to pour it into? They looked the same.

I felt her anticipation, waiting once again for me to make a mistake. Why did I feel such panic? The bitter taste of bile rose in my throat. How could she still have such power over me when I'd been gone from home for twenty years?

The steady drumming of her heart monitor calmed my jangled nerves and reminded me of how little power she had over me, except to make me feel pain.

I stared at the two cups by her bed. *Please, God, don't let me pour it into the wrong cup.* I swallowed over the burgeoning lump in my throat, tilted the can, and poured the fizzing liquid into the cup nearest Mama's hospital bed.

She clenched her teeth. "Not that one, stupid!"

Mama didn't realize she was two weeks from death, but even if she had, she still would have made me feel unloved. I despised the power she still held over me. She was dying, and I still detested her. As a mother myself, I would never treat my children the way she'd treated me. I turned and raced from the room.

Downstairs in the lobby, my husband waited with our four children. I fell into his arms, sobbing.

Most children gain self-worth from their mothers, but I'd received a legacy of pain and derision. From the time I was little, she had called me stupid. That word followed me throughout my school years, even into high school.

I was fifteen when my youngest sister was born, and Mama had promised I could go to the hospital for the birth. After arriving home from school that day, in all my exuberance, I tripped over a stool by the door.

Mama hollered, "Watch out, stupid!" and left me at home.

So many years later, on the way home from visiting her in the hospital that day, I knew I needed to forgive my mother. In Romans 12:17-18 the Bible tells us: *Do not repay anyone evil for evil. Be careful to do what is right in the eyes of everyone. If it is possible, as far as it depends on you, live at peace with everyone.*

But how? My heart still boiled with anger after the Coke incident.

I turned to God's Word, finding comfort in the Psalms. I read them all that week, sitting beside Mama's hospital bed. One day, I opened the Bible and read John 16:33: *I have told you these things, so that in me you may have peace. In this world you will have trouble. But take heart! I have overcome the world.*

His words became a soothing balm for my deepest and darkest wounds.

The peace Jesus talked about came through forgiveness. I had sat beside Mama's bed and allowed anger to envelop me, but Jesus' words pierced me like a knife. I had to let the anger go. My first step was to ask for forgiveness of my own sin before I could forgive my mother. No matter what she had done, I, too, stood guilty before God. I closed my eyes, releasing the most painful moments in my life to Him.

Father, I know I am a sinner. It's painfully clear to me. I'm asking You to forgive me for the anger I have toward my mother. Release me from this, Lord. Grant me Your peace, so I may be able to tell my mother goodbye.

It was almost impossible to imagine that God loved me when my own mother didn't. But that day, while reading my Bible, a passage leapt off the page. *How great is the love the Father has lavished on us, that we should be called children of God! And that is what we are!* (1 John 3:1).

God was speaking to me! Yes! I was His child — His daughter — and He loved me very much.

Through these conversations with Him, I began my journey of trust. Knowing and trusting God helped me listen for His promptings. Only in a quiet place in my heart would I hear a gentle word from Him.

Shortly before Mama died, I felt His prompting: *Tell her you love her.* Those words plumbed the depths of my soul. With God's peace blanketing me I stood beside my mother, struggling to form words of love and forgiveness we both needed to hear.

Her breathing turned ragged beneath the pale-green oxygen mask. The morphine had done its job — her eyes looked vacant. I didn't think she would hear me, but knew I must speak them anyway.

I lifted her hand and held it gently in mine. "Mama, I love you."

For a moment her hazel eyes cleared and locked on mine. A weak smile crept onto her lips.

Though I couldn't change Mama's attitude, through God's power, I could change my own. When I forgave Mama, I released her from what she'd done to me. And best of all, I released and forgave myself.

7

Forgiveness

Bob Blundell

The ancient steps that I stood upon were cracked with wrinkled veins of age. Each splintered line a reflection of times and events in history that I prayed would never be forgotten. This holy place overlooked the foothills that surrounded the historic City of David and Jerusalem beyond. The view was an oxymoronic blend of ancient alabaster structures, built centuries before Christ, contrasted against modern buildings standing straight and tall along the horizon. It was a testament to the harmony between old and new. And of how much the world had changed, yet in many ways remained the same.

As a sudden gust of wind swept across the great Temple kicking up a cloud of chalk-colored dust, I pulled my jacket up around my neck in defense of the bite and closed my eyes, taking myself back in time. After a few moments, the modern sounds around me became muffled voices that eventually faded into silence. I imagined how it may have been over two thousand years ago, on these same steps on the Mount of Olives where Jesus taught.

Slowly the images began to form, and I smiled as I saw the people gathered around Him. I could see their looks of joy and wonder at the message that He carried and of the miracles He had performed. And then. I felt myself there among them.

* * *

He was clad in an ash colored robe with a simple gold sash tied at his waist, and a brown woven shawl that hung over His broad and sturdy shoulders. His shoulder length hair was the color of cinnamon, and as He turned His face to speak to the people crowded around Him, the fading sunlight glistened on His long mane like shiny strands of gold.

Men, a dozen or more of many ages, stood around Him in a circle. Others sat on the steps near His feet, quietly watching, nodding in silent agreement and peering at Him with looks of amazement. The gentle warmth in His dark mahogany eyes seemed to speak to me and I watched Him, mesmerized by His presence.

But then, loud, frantic voices erupted near the eastern entrance. I looked down to see a boisterous crowd of a dozen or more coming up the steps. And stumbling ahead of them was a tall, raven-haired woman clad in a ripped and tattered ivory tunic. Two men shoved her through the entrance of the Temple as many others behind them shouted and cried out, pumping their fists in the air.

I could see a thin line of blood on her cheek and as she stumbled forward, two men, tall and muscular, gripped her frail arms lifting her up when she fell.

I watched as they dragged the woman, limp and bleeding, up the uneven steps. When they reached the top, they dropped her near His feet. He leaned down and gently stroked her head, as a mother would soothe a frightened child.

"Why have you seized this poor woman?" He asked, standing before the angry crowd.

As His words seemed to hang motionless in the crisp air, a sudden gust of wind swept across the Temple steps creating a cloud of dust that hovered like a dense fog around the feet of the angry men. Thunder rumbled ominously as angry slate-colored clouds moved quickly across the horizon and blocked out the fading sunlight.

The mob was cast in a blanket of darkness as if day had suddenly changed to night. Gasps and frightened whispers swept among them. But the Man stood alone; bathed in a bright shaft of light that pierced the sky. A radiant hue hovered around Him like a mist, making His eyes shine like burning embers in a fire.

Many of the men withdrew in fear. But an elder clad in splendid colors stepped forward to face the Man. His beard as white as the sandstone steps he stood upon, his hair hanging in long curls like lamb's wool, he spoke in a loud authoritative voice.

"Teacher! This woman has been caught in adultery. The law of Moses says she must be punished!"

He knelt and picked up a round, grey stone the size of a lemon and held it up in the air. "The laws of our fathers say she must be stoned to death!" As he finished these words, the men behind him began to scream loudly, yelling and shaking their fists in anger.

"Kill the adulteress," one shouted.

"Stone her!" cried another.

I watched as the angry cries continued to grow louder and louder, then the Teacher calmly knelt and began making signs in the dust with his finger. The voices calmed to hushed murmurs, the men intrigued by His actions.

"What is he doing?" one cried out.

"What is he writing?" another asked.

Then He stood and stepped toward the crowd, pointing at the woman who lay curled at His feet. "Let anyone among you who is without sin, be first to throw a stone at her."

There was silence at first, then a cacophony of confused voices. But the cries ceased when He knelt again and began to write in the dust. Several of the older men in the mob pressed forward to see what manner of words this man wrote. The ancient one who had spoken of the stoning was the first to see the writing. As he read the words formed in the dirt, his face suddenly turned ashen and the grey rock in his fist fell to the ground and clattered down the steep steps of the Temple. He slowly turned and walked away. Then sounds of other stones falling to the ground, one after another, broke the silence as slowly, one by one, the other men followed the elder.

As the crowd began to disperse, the Teacher lifted the woman to her feet. He brushed twisted strands of hair from her face and used his thumb to gently wipe blood from a cut below her eye.

I could see in His eyes, an incredible intensity that gleamed like stars in the evening sky. His smile shone with a warmth like that of a father's loving embrace. Then He and the woman spoke to one another. And after a moment she fell to her knees weeping and kissed His sandaled feet.

The people still gathered around who had seen and heard watched Him move toward the entrance below them. Minutes later, even though He could no longer be seen, the power of His simple words still floated like a fine mist among us. And all who had been there to witness, knew they would never be the same.

* * *

I opened my eyes to see the amber haze of the sun as it had begun its melt into the surrounding hills. Modern day sounds and voices began to fill the air again. Yet part of me still clung to the vision of that scene two thousand years ago. I didn't want to leave that incredible moment in time. It was a reminder that though we are all desperately flawed and in need of forgiveness, He will always be there to lift us to our feet, wipe the blood from our faces, and grant us His mercy.

8

Bunk Bed Blunder

Annmarie B. Tait

For a full twenty minutes I begged my older sister to trade bunks with me for one measly night. I had to know the thrill of sleeping in the top bunk bed or I would die of disappointment. Life is just that dramatic when you're eight years old.

My sister, the self-appointed president of the secret Do-Gooders Club, was not so all-fired sure that this was such a great idea. After all, Mom was no stranger to my appetite for adventure, and more than once she warned me to stay away from the top bunk.

Eventually my sister gave in to me on the pinky promise condition that I never, ever, as long as I drew breath, speak a word to Mom about our shenanigans. "Deal" I said, with a grin that stretched from one earlobe to the other.

After supper I attacked my homework with the speed of a gazelle. With that behind me, I ripped off my clothes, jumped into the tub, donned my jammies, then flopped into Daddy's comfy chair. That's where I waited, and waited, and waited for Ricky Nelson to sing "Travelin' Man" or some other hit which signaled the end of the *Ozzie and Harriet* show . . . and the start of my bedtime escapade. I bounded up the staircase two at a time.

"You didn't forget, did you?"

"No," my sister said, "but I still don't think it's a good idea."

"I don't care," I shot back in a panic. "You promised!"

All evening I had imagined the top bunk bed as a flying carpet upon which I could dash off to Disneyland, a cowboy ranch, the circus, or anywhere I wanted. I imagined it as a tree house, a hot air balloon like the one I'd seen in the *Wizard of Oz*, and a magical flying unicorn.

One thing was for sure, I'd never get anywhere unless I got myself up into that top bunk with the lights out before my two oldest sisters came to bed, found me out, and blew the lid off my little caper.

Our bunk beds, purchased at the local Army Navy surplus store, were made of gray steel that Mom had painted white. They were not equipped with an adorable little ladder like the maple bunk beds I saw advertised in the Sears catalog. Launching to the top was strictly up to the strength and dexterity of the occupant.

To get me up there my sister stood bent over, with her fingers laced together. I stepped into the cradle of her hands with one foot, grabbed the top bunk, and hoisted myself up while she pushed me at the same time. It wasn't very graceful but it got me to my destination all the same. Hardly had I made to the land of Oz on my flying magical unicorn when wouldn't you know it? I fell fast asleep.

The real excitement didn't start until well after midnight when I woke up with an urge to get to the bathroom . . . quickly! With a sleepy yawn I threw back the covers, swung my legs over the side, and stepped off into thin air plummeting to the floor with one loud thud. That sure woke me — and everybody else in the house in a hurry.

Mom and Daddy ran to our bedroom with all speed. When they arrived, Daddy picked me up off the floor and my sister scooted over in the lower bunk. Then Daddy gently put me down next to her. I never complained, cried, or said a single thing except, "I'm so sorry."

My mother bent over and kissed me, asking if I was all right. I answered, "Fine. I'm fine. I'm so sorry."

She just whispered, "Go to sleep now."

Mom never scolded me. She never so much as reminded me of her warning to stay away from the top bunk bed.

When the commotion settled down my sister asked me if I was really okay. "I'm not sure," I said. "My arm hurts a little. I'll probably be okay in the morning."

She drifted off to sleep and I lay there filled with shame. My arm throbbed and I never closed my eyes the rest of the night.

As daybreak approached, I saw my navy blue school uniform with a freshly pressed uniform blouse hanging on the hook where my mother had left it for me. I knew I would never put it on that day. When I saw daylight I woke my sister and asked her to go get Mom for me.

My mother arrived and sat down on the bed next to me and the tears I had held in all night long now flowed freely. "I don't think I can move my arm," I said between sniffles.

"Why didn't you tell me last night?" She smoothed my long brown hair away from my eyes.

"Because I'm so ashamed." By then I was sobbing.

Mom didn't drive, and Daddy had long since left for work. So, after she dressed me we trudged three blocks to the bus stop. The bus was crowded with people going to work. She stood next to me with her arm around my shoulder to steady me as best she could as the bus rumbled down the street.

When we arrived in the Emergency Room a nurse whisked me off to the X-ray Department. As we waited together for the x-ray results, Mom put her arm around me and assured me that everything would be okay. The ice pack the nurse gave me kept sliding off my arm but my mother held it in place and spoke softly to calm me down.

When all was said and done, we learned my wrist was fractured. A plaster cast was applied from my knuckles clear up over my elbow. What a day!

On the way home from the hospital we got off the bus two stops early and went into the Five-and-Ten where there was a lunch counter. The butter pecan ice cream they served was top notch and we ordered two cones. Somewhere between licks I summoned the courage to ask why I didn't get in trouble for sleeping in the top bunk.

Mom said, "You didn't need any lecture from me. Your conscience took care of that. What you needed was someone's hand to hold, someone's shoulder to cry on, and someone to buy you an ice cream cone when the whole thing was behind you."

We walked home from the Five-and-Ten store nice and slow, soliciting sympathy galore from anyone who spotted my arm in a plaster cast, resting in a brand new white cotton sling.

I remember that special day with my mom when it is on the tip of my tongue to say "I told you so" to someone already suffering the consequences of a poor choice.

I think twice and then suggest we go get an ice cream cone.

9

Loose Threads

Patricia Ritsema

Though one can be overpowered, two can defend themselves.
A cord of three strands is not quickly broken.
Ecclesiastes 4:12

In my pain, after the death of my husband, the expression "hanging on by a thread" took on a whole new meaning. I felt like my life had been dealt a blow leaving a gaping hole with loose threads unraveling. The main thread of my life`s long story appeared to be severed.

Our marriage had been based on the Bible's three-strand concept, the thread comprised of John, me, and God. God was the strand that tied us together. Now that my husband was missing, the three-strand image seemed broken, leaving me unwinding and unraveling.

I remembered reading a Chinese legend that maintained that there is a red thread which binds together loved ones, such as our friends, our families, and all those we consider important in our lives. That red thread legend reminded me of another thread story: The British Royal Navy's ropes had a distinctive red strand running through the middle to serve as a reminder that the rope belonged to the Crown.

The image of the red thread comforted me. As I considered those ropes belonging to the Royal Navy, my thoughts moved to us belonging to the Royal Family of God. I could visualize family, friends, my husband and me all bound together by the red thread of His love. This image reminds me that we belong to Him and He is still the thread that ties us together.

Our life tapestry is woven with threads of joy and sorrow, brightness and darkness, bitter and sweet in various hues and intensities.

Corrie ten Boom, Christian author, speaker, and survivor of World War II's Ravensbrück concentration camp, wrote a well-loved poem *Life Is But the Weaving | The Tapestry Poem* about God weaving the threads of our life into a tapestry. She shared that we cannot choose the colors and we can only see the messy underside of that tapestry while He sees the uppers side as His skillful hand uses dark threads as well as silver and gold to weave the pattern of our life that He has planned.

Our God became man so that He could redeem the broken strands in us and in our world. The Father, Son, and Holy Spirit are like a cord holding us together. We were woven together, body, soul and spirit, to live forever with faith, hope and love.

* * *

Father, give us the wisdom to trust You as we learn the skill of accepting life's varied threads — the harsh advance of age, the pangs of grief, the loss of family and friends, the loss of clarity — and with fresh insight embrace them as a part of a rich and elegant pattern combined with the joy and beauty you place in and around us.

Please give us the grace to take the whole of life in all its hues — the dark and the bright — and allow you to be the Weaver of all the loose threads into a beautiful tapestry that gives You glory and honor. Amen

Overcome

Nancy Kelley Alvarez

My excitement knew no bounds when my husband and I adopted "Pete," an eleven-year-old Filipino boy. When we discovered we could not have our own children, adoption became our hope. At long last, our home would be filled with laughter and love.

After three years Pete began running away, leaving me with crushing disillusionment. Pete disappeared eleven times in one year. The last time he was gone for a month. To further complicate things, this happened in Manila, a metropolis of twelve million where the police force is spread too thin to track runaway children.

Dazed, I could barely focus.

Long conversations with the Lord usually began with a host of questions: Where did we go wrong? Why are You allowing this to happen? Didn't we try everything to help him? Was I too strict? Not strict enough? The shame, anger and disappointment adhered like thick mud, pushing me to the verge of depression. The accusations still reverberate in my mind.

How I long for a dramatic ending, proving God's great power; but so far that hasn't happened. Although we eventually found him, Pete moved out of our house at sixteen, his empty room a constant reminder of my failure.

Through it all, I did not doubt God's love. I searched His Word for answers. After many months, I came upon Romans 12:21: *Do not be overcome by evil, but overcome evil with good.*

Bam! The verse came alive. The slippery slope of loss developed into a journey of discovery. A co-worker recommended a book on the oppression women face today throughout the world. As I devoured it, my pain paled in comparison to what many experience.

The Lord infused me with a desire to turn my pain into overcoming evil with good. While I can't force Pete to live for Jesus, I can bless others experiencing their own stories of sorrow.

I asked the Lord for an opportunity to help oppressed women, especially victims of human trafficking. After much perseverance, a door opened for me to volunteer with sexually exploited victims. In a city that at the time was noted for having the world's worst traffic, I needed to get up at 4:30 A.M. in order to arrive for the weekly 7 A.M. devotion time. As an introvert, I felt way out of my comfort zone. I didn't know if I could build good rapport with these thirty women.

Throughout the next four years, I became deeply committed to the young women as we laughed and cried together, sharing our joys and heartaches. I told stories of women from the Bible — Hagar, Sarah, Esther, and others — who experienced both cruelty and God's love. When I asked the women what they learned from these stories, they said, "Never give up. There's always hope. God loves me. God has a good plan for me." A hallelujah chorus erupted in my heart.

My time with these women gave me a safe community. I needed them, too. As we struggled to make sense of our grief, I gained a deeper awareness of God's love for women and His intense commitment to rescue us in the midst of the world's ugliness.

With the Lord's help, I will continue to conquer sin with good and shine His light in the darkness (Philippians 2:15). He isn't through with me, or our son. My fluttering emotions can drag me into despair or tug me closer to Jesus. It's my decision.

I can't control my son's choices. However, I can refuse to let ugly emotions imprison me. As I see women around me transformed by His Word, I gain more faith that God can work in the lives of those I love.

When I help shoulder others' burdens, joy wraps around me, releasing me from the lies the evil one uses to taunt me. I hope my son will live a godly life soon. In the meantime, I will give thanks for the opportunity to comfort others.

While I would never have chosen this journey of pain, it's what God has chosen for me. I can either resist or receive it. I pray the Lord will be glorified as I welcome the hurting into my heart.

God can take a broken heart and turn it into a compassionate one that overcomes evil with good.

11

Testing One, Two, Three...

Ashley Dutch

Among the sounds I like best are children's voices lifted in songs of worship. In fact, I enjoy it so much, I decided to lead the children's singing group at our local church.

What the group of ten to fifteen members lacked in quantity, they made up for in dedication.

We met to practice songs we would later sing in a special performance in the sanctuary for the adult service. Week after week we practiced the songs, but I couldn't help but be nervous about the performance. Would the sound system play the music and not the voices on the DVD? Did the children know all the words? Would all of the children show up to sing? Would they sing loud enough?

As question after question flooded my mind, I felt this question from God: *Who are you putting on a show for?*

Each week as we came closer to the performance date, I could still hear this question in my mind. My response was, "You God, these songs are for you!"

Then why are you so worried about a perfect performance for others?

I thought of the verse in Galatians: *Am I now trying to persuade people, or God? Or am I striving to please people? If I were still trying to please people, I would not be a servant of Christ* (Galatians 1:10 csb).

I wish I could say that thinking of this scripture was enough to eliminate my anxieties, but in truth I still struggled as one issue after another popped up just a week or two before the performance. This child wasn't able to make it. That microphone wouldn't work.

The challenges continued.

Even though repeating the words "this is all for God" numerous times to myself, by the morning of the performance I was still stressed, to say the least.

The risers were set up, check. The microphones were working, check. The lights were on and would be spotlighting the children, check.

We were off to a good start. The children entered the sanctuary and stepped up onto the risers. No trips, no stumbles, no accidents. *Thank you God.* They stood proudly just waiting for the music to start. I stood waiting to direct them in song.

We waited.

We waited some more.

I walked over to the sound booth and did not like the look on the sound guy's face. Though we had tested it a half a million times, the DVD would not play. He checked to see if it were cracked or broken. Regardless of the reason, there would be no music for the children to sing with. I panicked! *Now what?* I looked out over the sanctuary as everyone looked on with anticipation for their beautiful little gifts from God to sing an uplifting worship song.

My eyes turned from the crowd to the children becoming antsy and not-so-patiently waiting for the music to start. I released a heavy sigh as I made my way to the children to inform them of the situation. I asked them if they felt they could sing without any music at all. That was the only idea I had left. With a few blank nervous stares and plenty of hesitation, the children nodded and agreed to try.

I smiled and reminded them to have fun and remember to Whom we were singing. I turned to the crowd, took a microphone and admitted our predicament. I became teary as I announced that these children had worked so hard and were willing to sing without their music.

I returned the microphone, faced the children and we began to sing.

Now, I am not going to say it was flawless; yet though far from perfect, they did a wonderful job and the congregation cheered. I truly believe God smiled.

I learned a lesson that day. In what we may think is a ruined or broken moment, God is in control and we have to trust Him, knowing He is not looking for the best production.

It's not about the songs, the lights, the sound system, or how great a voice we have. It's not about the show, the number of people, what we wear, or how all-together we are.

It's about our hearts, our worship. It's about why we worship. It's about God, and His son dying on the cross for us. It's about building His kingdom and bringing Him glory. And I am so grateful for any opportunity to be a part of it.

12

Is This It?

Kathleen Kohler

Our granddaughters pirouetted in the lobby of Seattle's Macaw Hall, noting whose dress flared in a perfect swirl. Nearby our three grandsons, dressed in suits and ties, slouched on green velvet chairs. When the doors opened the boys hopped up, joining the crowd being ushered into the theater. Seated inside, the audience fell silent as the lights dimmed and the orchestra played the overture. Several minutes into the music, never having attended a ballet, our grandson Chase whispered into the dark. "Is this it?"

I chuckled to myself, but before I could answer him the curtains rose. A spotlight shined down on an old fashioned Christmas scene as *The Nutcracker* ballet commenced.

"Oh . . ." Chase gasped.

Mesmerized throughout the performance, Chase reveled in the clash between the mouse king and the prince. When the cannon blasted during their infamous battle, Chase nearly jumped out of his seat.

Like the performance hall, sometimes life appears so dark we can't see a solution to the problems we face. Yet backstage, behind the curtain, people are gearing up for their grand entrance. A spotlight floods the stage. The curtain opens and a fanciful story unfolds.

Whether it's our own challenges or those of people we know or read about, we often ask the same question as eight-year-old Chase.

Is this it?

* * *

In 1 Kings 17:8-16 I read about a widow with just enough food to prepare one last meal. Seeing no future in their bleak circumstances, she resigned herself and her son to death. But God had a different plan. Filled with compassion for her plight, God sent Elijah to her rescue. The result? A miracle of an endless supply of flour and oil.

In my own life, twelve weeks after cancer ended my dad's fight, six weeks after our daughter suffered a devastating blow to her marriage, I received a somber phone call from my husband. "Doug's (my brother) been in an accident. They don't know yet if he'll make it."

Blackened skies shrouded the Seattle skyline as I stared out a rain-pelted window from the fourth-floor hospital room. My brother, and only sibling, groaned in a sedated sleep. Minute by minute, hour after hour, the clock ticked as I shifted my position in a hard plastic chair.

In thirteen short weeks I had gone from the joyous August birth of our grandson Chase to a blinding grief. Baffled by not just one, but multiple tragic events, silent tears stained my cheeks. I whispered, "Lord, is this it? Is this the plan?"

Darkness pervaded the future, but God was at work in ways I couldn't see.

Though my brother lost the use of his right arm and was never able to resume work, he did survive.

His recovery was a long, grueling process. Being right handed he had to retrain himself to write with his left hand, and even today he battles chronic pain.

On a trip to the grocery store the following June, he eyed a display of Bing cherries. Ripping a produce bag from the roll he could already taste the sweet cherry juice. He attempted to wrestle open the plastic bag with his one good hand, but no matter how he tried he couldn't separate the bag's sides. Defeated, he gave up and left the store.

My heart ached for him when he told me what happened. Not only could he no longer run the business he had started right out of high school, he couldn't open a produce bag.

A self-reliant man, he had to learn to ask for help.

While navigating these changes he met new people in the community. With a woman he met, he attended church for the first time in decades. She brought a light into his world, and after months of dating he proposed. The pastor of the little church performed an outdoor, summer wedding. Our family rejoiced that at fifty-four my brother married for the first time, and embarked on a whole new adventure.

A few years earlier, when I had thought his life might end, it was as if God said, "Wait, his story isn't over." Like Chase in the darkened theater and the widow staring into empty cupboards, the Lord drew back a heavy curtain and my brother realized a future he never expected.

Ashley's Story

Cheryl A. Paden

I met Ashley when I joined a yoga class. As we became better acquainted, we learned we were both Christians who wanted healthy lifestyles. I was impressed by her story of a changed life, and with her permission I wrote it.

* * *

"Have you ever tried God?" a coworker asked Ashley, as he walked over to her desk at the bank.

Why is this guy asking me this? Is the stress I feel showing on my face?

Ashley never imagined what a difference one question would have on her life.

Sure she'd dabbled in Christianity. In high school she had joined her friends and attended church. She'd gone to worship on Sunday mornings, and some youth activities, but it had been all about the rules, not a relationship. She'd decided it didn't work. Besides the path she had taken did not include God anymore. God would not be able to fix the problems she had now.

God could not make her three year old not be autistic. God could not fix her failing marriage or her financial worries.

Ashley needed alcohol, cigarettes, and food to help her relax and get through the tough stuff life threw at her. She liked her party girl image. Life was more carefree. Drinking meant no worries, forgetting heartaches, and escaping problems.

But her drinking didn't really solve problems; it created more. Problems like overspending, late nights, destructive relationships, and bad choices.

"Will you come to church with me? Just try," the coworker encouraged.

Ashley agreed, although worried that the church people would judge her and her lifestyle choices. What would they think of an alcoholic divorcee who broke the rules she had learned in her teen years? One who smoked, drank, cursed and had tattoos.

However, this church experience wasn't like that. These people taught her about having a relationship with Christ. She began participating in Bible studies that emphasized redemption in Christ and breaking free from the past to live a life with hope.

In the beginning she might pick up a couple of beers and go work on her Bible study, but Ashley discovered that as her relationship with Christ deepened, her desire for addictions lessoned. She quit drinking and smoking and everything began to change.

Lord, you brought me out of this. I am so thankful. What can I do for you? Ashley prayed. God began opening doors and revealed a new life for Ashley. Her healthy-living journey began with small steps.

The first change happened when she participated in a DAN (Defeat Autism Now) program for her son. The program emphasized not eating packaged foods, but eating from the earth as God had designed. God created the apple, not frozen pastries, to nourish our bodies. Not only did her son's health improve, but her health did as well as she dropped unwanted pounds.

Ashley felt a lot of stress being a single parent raising a special needs child. She read that exercise was good for stress, so she decided to try. Stepping into a yoga class she wondered how their philosophy would match up with her Bible study and Christian teachings. She found the deep breathing and stretching exercises were calming and had a health benefit.

As time went on, Ashley studied people and recognized many who were struggling with different types of addictions, diets that lacked nutrition, and couch-potato lifestyles. In her Midwestern community people identified themselves as Christians, yet as many as seventy-five percent could be considered overweight, even obese.

Why isn't the church talking about this? she wondered.

God replied, *Because I am asking you to respond.*

As Ashley continued to pray, her new life emerged. She focused on how to motivate others to healthy living: a lifestyle that honors Christ. Scripture confirmed her philosophy, *Whether you eat or drink or whatever you do, do it all for the glory of God* (1 Corinthians 10:31).

Ashley developed a yoga program called "Spirit Flow" for Christians. The group met at a church. Each class began with a devotional, followed with yoga exercises and ended with prayer. The class played Christian background music and participants were reminded that their breath, their bodies, and their lives are a gift from God.

As Spirit Flow's success continued the participants began asking for more — a deeper and more intense class. From their feedback, and working with a friend, Ashley developed the Connect program. This two-hour Christ centered class ran for seven weeks, designed to include a full hour of Bible study and a full hour of yoga exercise.

Today Ashley does not have to wonder where her life might have ended if she had continued down her former path. Her husband is a counselor for drug and alcohol addicts and she knows the tragedy of an addict's life.

Ashley continues to look forward. She hopes to expand her Connect program and ministry to a larger audience. As a part of that goal, she started a blog about her journey at whole-ministries.com.

"I know that teaching others about healthy living is how I am called to serve God," she says. "I am so thankful God brought me here."

Ashley is living proof of how a broken life can become whole again, and an example of 2 Corinthians 5:17: *If anyone is in Christ, he is a new creation; the old has gone, the new has come.*

14

Growing Pains

Norma C. Mezoe

I stood upon the mountain top
and viewed the world below . . .
My spirit was elated
and filled with rosy glow.

Then I returned to the valley,
because the Lord commanded, "Go!"
For it's in the deepest valleys
where our spirits truly grow.

Mountain tops are wonderful,
They make our spirits glow . . .
But it's in the deepest valleys
Where our spirits truly grow.

A Hard-Learned Lesson

Diana C. Derringer

Discretion will protect you, and understanding will guard you.
Proverbs 2:11

Head down, shoulders shaking, and tears flowing — this was not the jovial Uncle Leonard we had known.

Years of poor choices still showed in the crevices of his bony face. However, his wrinkles no longer widened with laughter that turned into a ragged cough. He wasn't regaling us with another of his drunken escapades, like the middle-of-the-night trip from Indiana to Kentucky when he realized he was driving the wrong way. He wasn't doubled over, slapping his legs, as he described heading north on I-65 while all the headlights shined south toward him.

Neither was he recalling childhood memories or catching up on extended-family's news with our mother. Gone was the confident man who discussed the economy, work details, or the latest ballgame with our father.

Uncle Leonard sat before us, a broken man.

Learning the Hard Way

Never a mean alcoholic, Uncle Leonard emanated a love for life and others despite his addiction. We rarely knew when he was coming. He simply showed up at any hour to stay a day, a week, or several months when he sought sobriety. He knew drinking was prohibited at our house.

However, he also knew he was welcome any time and in any condition for however long it took to regain a clearer mind and healthier body.

He had fallen off the wagon once again, but this time was different. As he sat across the kitchen table from my younger sister and me, his yellowed fingers danced as he raised them for another puff of courage.

Sweating sorrow, he begged, "Girls, please listen to your old uncle. I've made so many mistakes. I didn't mean to end up like this." His head bobbed to his chest and then up again. Following several blows into his handkerchief, plus a couple of swipes at his eyes, he continued. "I love you. You know that, don't you?"

We nodded, and he kept talking. "Promise me you'll never take that first drink. Please, look at me. Listen to me. You don't want to live like this." He spread his arms wide, the leathered skin hanging on his skinny frame. His eyes reflected broken relationships and missed opportunities.

We did listen and never forgot the lessons from this gentle, hard-working man who loved us with his entire being but suffered the demons of a bottle tipped time after time.

Eventually, by remaining near the support of our father and others in his small but close-knit support system, Uncle Leonard managed to listen to his own advice. He held on to sobriety, remarried, reignited his relationship with God, and bought a house not far from ours. He lived well and laughed often until the day of his early death, a consequence of one drink that led to many.

Learning a Better Way

In addition to learning from Uncle Leonard's mistakes, we learned from our parents who supported, confronted, and guided Uncle Leonard to a better way of life. My sister and I took the way they lived for granted. Looking back, we see the impact they made and the example they set for us and anyone else who visited or lived with us.

Relatives, friends, and foster children found food, shelter, love, and spiritual guidance when they resided under our roof. Church attendance, family devotions before bedtime, and prayers before meals were the norm. Mom and Dad coupled unconditional love with firm standards for behavior.

Those childhood lessons from Uncle Leonard and our parents continue to guide us today. We thank them for their love and care.

16

Lessons from Eggs and Eggshells

Nate Stevens

God is the Judge: He puts down one, and exalts another.
Psalm 75:7 NKJV

Eggshells and scrambled eggs are a horrible combination.

While making breakfast, I cracked three eggs and poured their contents into the frying pan. As I tossed the final eggshell into the trash, an interesting thought struck me. Before cracking the shell and spilling the actual egg white and yoke, the shell is a valuable and inseparable part of the egg. It serves its purpose by safeguarding and delivering the egg. Without it, the egg becomes a slimy mess, probably unsafe for eating.

However, by breaking the shell, it becomes disposable. When the purpose is accomplished, separation becomes necessary.

In life, everything serves a purpose. The box delivering a gift. Our bodies upon release of our spirits. Even friends along the journey, while joined in purpose, are indispensable. However, once their purpose is accomplished, God may move them to separate journeys. Some friends help us through struggles while others cause them. Some friends stick by us through thick and thin while others sever relationships over petty arguments or disagreements.

Aside from questioning motives, faithfulness, and character, it is vital to understand how God sovereignly uses every instance of life for His ultimate purpose. He lifts one up while putting another down (Psalm 75:7). He brings people into our lives while removing others. Sometimes He forcefully loosens our grasp on those things and people He knows no longer serve His purpose or our long-term good. But if we approach such scenarios with an egg and eggshell mentality, we soon realize keeping an empty eggshell is pointless. It served its purpose — time to let go and move on.

This should not encourage a frivolous or callous approach toward friendships or a devaluation of the people in our lives. It reinforces recognition of God's sovereign control. He allows eggs and eggshells to coexist until such time as the egg moves on while the eggshell does not. He calls some people to journeys with forks of separation in the road.

Crunching an overlooked piece of broken eggshell in my scrambled eggs emphasizes clean separation is necessary. However, such separation should occur with much discernment and without discord, dissension, or disrespect.

Lord, grant me the gratitude for the eggs in my life, the courage to discard the eggshells, and Your discernment to tell the difference.

17

Broken Shards of Redemption

Lynn Mosher

The young boy walked the path several times a day. His bare feet squished in the mud as he walked along this narrow lane to get water, go to school, and forage for food.

Rain had drenched all the paths and roads, making them sloppy and hard to travel in and out of the impoverished village.

A small, burlap bag, tied with an old piece of cloth, hung from the belt loop of his ripped pants. Each day, he walked through the village and picked up fragments of broken colored glass and put them in the bag.

The boy thought of himself as being just like those discarded shards — having no purpose — but he also thought, *Someday, I'll make something beautiful out of these broken pieces of glass.*

Then one day, a missionary scheduled to speak at the small church in the boy's village arrived at the nearby airport and felt led to buy a book — one of no interest to him.

Though puzzled, he bought it.

On the first Sunday, the missionary preached on the worth God sees in each life. The boy listened intently as the missionary taught how God takes all the broken pieces of each life and turns them into something beautiful. Something with purpose, for God's glory.

When the service was over, the missionary felt led to give the book to the boy, who was grateful but perplexed as to what he would do with a book titled *How to Make a Stained Glass Window.*

After the missionary left, the boy began reading the book, which triggered an idea. He wrote a letter to the missionary asking a favor.

When the missionary received the letter, he rushed to send a package in answer to the boy's request.

Rainy season had already begun. A few days before the missionary's package arrived, a storm swept through the village and a falling a tree broke a window in the little church.

Unfortunately, no funds existed to fix the window. Church members feared more rain would pour through the opening and ruin the church. So, they covered the opening the best they could.

When the missionary's package arrived, the boy gathered all of his broken pieces of colored glass, moved them around to form a pattern, and soon fashioned what he thought was a lovely design with a cross.

He worked day and night to adhere the pieces.

As he worked, he kept repeating one verse the missionary had quoted from Romans 8:28 (NLT): *We know that God causes everything to work together for the good of those who love God and are called according to his purpose for them.*

The Lord whispered to him, "As the artist works, he unites the pieces of glass together, redeeming them into a beautiful work of art. So it is with your life. I work to bond your broken fragments together, uniting them for good, redeeming them into something beautiful."

When the boy had finished his work, he took the window to the pastor, who was deeply grateful and praised the boy's work.

Members of the church helped install the window while there was a lull in the rain.

The next Sunday, the boy went to church, excited to see his beautiful shards of redemption in place. He slowly walked in and, overwhelmed at the sight, fell to his knees, lifting his hands to praise the Lord.

A ray of sun filtered through stunning hues of colored glass fragments, casting an image of the cross across the young boy's face . . . and his heart.

Tears streamed down his cheeks, for he now knew God had blessed him and had fit all his broken pieces together, redeeming him. He carried these words in his heart thereafter.

I am no longer broken. I am redeemed.
Now, I have worth and a purpose. For God's glory.

Do we know we have worth and beauty and a purpose? Do we know God will redeem all the shards of our life, making us into something beautiful for His glory?

May we always know how valuable and worthy we are!

18

Redirected by a (Heavenly) Father's Love

Diana L. Flegal

Between my Junior and Senior year of high school, I fell in love with a boy I met at a coffee house in my hometown. His name was Michael and he had the most luxurious long, black hair, and a terrific attitude on life. Each week, I strummed my guitar amidst the scent of patchouli and the smoke of candles stuck in old wine bottles. We sang songs like *We Are One in the Spirit* and *Jerimiah Was a Bullfrog*, along with *House of the Rising Sun*. Yes, we were all over the map.

Our country was in the middle of the Vietnam War and the US draft was a real threat. Best friends of my brother were over there fighting for something we couldn't understand. It was post Woodstock and people my age were seriously looking into the free love movement. Even Christian youth. After all, God was LOVE personified and we were created with certain drives (if you get my drift).

My friend Michael wanted to adopt a Conscientious Objector status to escape the draft and I happened to belong to a church denomination that had that status. So his mission became mine.

Our church had an established mission school and outreach in Lost Creek, Kentucky, and yes, they would appreciate our help the summer of 1970. Especially with their summer youth programs.

God knew our motives were not all pure and at the last minute, Michael and I broke up. I couldn't back out from going after our trip had been announced in the church bulletin; it would embarrass my parents and my church. So I packed my guitar and my Twiggy wig and best jeans, and off I went to Lost Creek.

Once I arrived, I saw Christ's love in action. Looking back now, I know the pastor discerned I was on my way down a prodigal's path. But these people loved me — the kids my age who had grown up in the mission compound, and the retired Mr. Hall, who had moved there to love on these kids for his remaining years. I felt the rocky foundation under my feet steady, even as I shared my above repertoire of songs.

Did I say, they loved me?

My bunk was in the girl's dorm and yes, we stayed up talking about boys and makeup. My heart connected with these incredible people. Beth, Pat, Janet and I became fast friends. They hadn't grown up with the privileges I had, yet their joy was palpable.

God was wooing me back to himself.

My first days there they took me around their world, introducing me to some people in town — where I saw the Hatfield and McCoy feud in action (scary stuff involving guns and hate-filled speech).

A July school field trip to Cincinnati, Ohio had been planned before I arrived so I was graciously included. Mr. Hall would drive the fourteen-passenger van, and we would take in a Cincinnati Reds and Pittsburgh Pirates baseball game. As a Pirates fan, I had heard all about Johnny Bench. I was happy I would get to see him play.

The van was packed with our lunches. The glass bottles in a large case of pop clanked together as we flew up the eight-lane highway. I remember Pat complaining once about our snacks getting caught in the braces on her teeth she'd just had cemented on the day before.

The game was fun and we were sunburned and tired when it was over. Mr. Hall headed the van toward home in the dark, and an usual silence filled the van as many of us dozed.

Our van was hit head on by a nineteen-year-old driving under the influence of alcohol. As I regained consciousness, I noticed how clear the windshield was and how bright the starlit sky. When I reached out to touch a low hanging star my hand went right through the windshield. As I turned my head, I saw Mr. Hall, so still and slumped over the steering wheel. Somehow, I knew he had passed away. Pat slumped next to me, dazed as well.

The sound of crying and moaning drew me to look to my left. All of the van's remaining passengers sat on a guardrail, lined up like birds on a wire. When Janet saw I was alive she hurried to my side, a tee shirt of one of the boys pressed to her mouth. The flying pop bottles had smashed her front teeth out of her mouth.

God, how could you let this happen to someone so loving as Mr. Hall, and to my new friends, and to me?

I screamed up toward the star-hung sky loudly as I could, "God, where are you?" and I saw a vision. A large hand reached down from heaven and into the van, and peace enveloped me like a blanket. It was hours until help arrived and cut me out of the van. The front end was smashed into my legs, and the rear seat was pressed up into my back. The engine, to my left, had burnt a hole in my leg. Mercifully, I drifted in and out of consciousness.

When I was finally placed in an ambulance, they took me to a clinic staffed by a male intern with longer hair than mine. He took my pulse with a pocket watch and told me he couldn't believe I hadn't bled out and the metal of the back seat hadn't severed my spine. Then he proceeded to cut off my favorite jeans!

I was transferred to the Lexington, Kentucky hospital and after four weeks in traction was placed in a body cast and flown to Pennsylvania by my dad's. My gurney fit right inside the small plane that had been refitted to carry Vietnam War dead.

Through the next year of my recovery — dealing with gangrene, having my leg rebroken to set it better, learning to walk again — I felt God's abiding presence.

I know now it was the Good Shepherd's mercy and great love that not only preserved my life, but also guided me back on a grace filled course.

19

Glory from Brokenness

Joanna Eccles

It never ceases to amaze me how God transforms things that seem to be leftovers into something magnificent.

The leader of my women's retreat started with the story of Jesus feeding the five thousand.

First, He asked His disciples to find food for what would have been over twenty thousand people with women and children included. The disciples looked at Jesus like He was crazy. Where were they going to find seven months' wages to buy that much food?

But Jesus insisted they feed the people. He knew they were tired and hungry. Jesus desired to meet their needs. So, Andrew brought a young lad with his humble lunch of five loaves of bread and two small fish to feed five thousand people.

Jesus took the bread and fish and blessed them. Then He broke the loaves and fish into pieces. From that, Jesus fed all of the people. Not only did everyone have enough, when Jesus sent His disciples to pick up the leftovers, twelve full baskets remained.

Jesus doesn't waste the broken parts. Actually, He loves those best. It is because the bread was broken that Jesus was able to feed so many.

The leader at our retreat acknowledged that sometimes in life we feel broken. Life comes at us unexpectedly and then . . . *Wham!*

To illustrate, she threw a plate on the floor. The sound echoed throughout the room. We sat there shocked, unsure what had happened. She explained that when life gets hard, we are shattered. Broken shards are everywhere. She picked up the parts from the floor, and noted how we try to gather the pieces we find and move along with what remains.

Then, life hits again . . . *Wham!*

She hurled the broken pieces down, resulting in more broken bits. Then she described how sometimes life is relentless and continues to pound us.

She pummeled that plate to smithereens with a wrench.

I could feel my heart pounding in my chest.

I tried to watch, but tears drenched my eyes. I was witnessing my life from the previous year.

My bad week that April was the first real crash. Dreams shattered, leaving me stunned. But I had picked up the pieces and marched forward.

Then things fell apart again, and the fall was worse.

Before I saw the leader's example, the way I described it was that I felt like a piñata that had once been colorful, holding sweet things inside. Then I'd been repeatedly bludgeoned with a baseball bat until all that remained was a tattered and empty shell.

I hurt.

God began to gather my pain and reconfigure it the same way the leader began to form those bits of plate into something on the floor. She made a mosaic from the fragments. Something that never could have formed had the plate not broken. When she completed the mosaic, it formed the word *glory*.

God loves broken people. He knows that includes each of us. Psalm 34:18 (NKJV) tells us *the Lord is near to those who have a broken heart, and saves such as have a contrite spirit.*

When we let Him, God takes all our hurt, all our suffering, our pain, and shame, and reworks them into something beautiful for His glory. He knows what to do with the fragmens that result from the hardship of living in a fallen world. God doesn't waste our pain.

God is doing that in my life now. I was in a lot of pain. I never imagined God would have me blog and podcast. He is giving me new dreams to replace the ones that died. Not that my original dreams were bad; they were too small. God has better ways to expand my borders to reach more people for His glory. But I had to be broken first.

God is teaching me not to resist when I'm broken, but to get excited. Because He loves to use the broken shards from our jars of clay and transform them for His glory.

20

A Delicate Pilgrimage

Lola Di Giulio Di Maci

When I was a child, I had a beautiful rosary with ruby-red glass beads that slipped through my fingers gracefully as I prayed. I loved that rosary — the color of it and the feel of it in my hands. But somewhere along the way, I lost it.

I looked everywhere for that rosary. I never found it.

Today I am feeling a much greater loss.

Years ago, my infant daughter quietly tiptoed into my life on a warm summer evening and then left as quickly as she came, seeing the light of only one morning. She was just nine hours and one-minute old — but in my heart, she had lived a lifetime. She was my third and last baby. I named her Angela.

Throughout the years, I have never forgotten the joy of seeing my baby's face when she miraculously came into my life. Our brief meeting went from tears of unspeakable joy and happiness to those of devastation and emptiness in a matter of minutes.

My road to recovery became a delicate pilgrimage of questionable paths I followed in trying to find my way back to a somewhat normal life without her. When I eventually came to realize that Angela was my baby — my daughter — no matter what, I began to heal.

On the thirty-eighth anniversary of her birth, I received an envelope in the mail from a Benedictine Abbey in Wisconsin. Inside was a beautiful rosary with ruby-red, glass beads, each bead in the shape of a perfect heart.

I felt that this was a sign, perhaps a gift, from my baby daughter, reaffirming what I had felt in my soul all along . . . that she had been there with me all the while.

As the first light of dawn announces the birth of each brand-new day, I run my fingers over the shiny glass beads of my ruby-red rosary, caressing each one in heartfelt gratitude for the precious gift of life.

And I am at peace.

21

Babysitting the Washing Machine

Beverly Varnado

The washing machine is overflowing again!" I cried out to my husband as I ran to the laundry room. We arrived at the machine at the same time to lift the lid in order to stop the water draining into the pipe behind the machine from spilling onto the floor.

I sighed and looked at my husband. "What are we going to do?"

I had babysat many times for children and pets, but I never thought I would have to spend my time babysitting a washing machine. For months, when it was running I had to make sure I was there when it emptied, so I could open the lid and allow the water to drain slowly into the plumbing so it wouldn't backflow onto the floor. This time, I'd gotten distracted and left the room. There was nothing wrong with the machine; the problem was the broken down old pipes in the house that had been built several decades ago.

The pipes probably needed to be replaced, but the resources to do such an extensive repair had yet to make their way into our bank account. So, we kept up the laundry vigil.

I mopped up the water on the floor and pondered our circumstances. By faith, we'd agreed to house a young couple, Landon and Brook, who needed a temporary place to stay. He worked for a restaurant chain, and they would travel the country for a couple of years training, but they had a few weeks' lapse between housing situations.

Through the years, we had opened our home to missionaries, ministry interns, and friends who needed a place to live. Some stayed as long as a year. We'd always felt it was part of our ministry.

However, recent financial reversals caused us to live more frugally than before, and sometimes we had to wait to make necessary repairs. The plumbing had fallen under that category.

But we couldn't really expect guests to do what we'd been doing with the washing machine, and they might not feel comfortable with me doing their laundry for them.

My husband and I have a habit of praying every night before we go to sleep. We pray for our family, church, friends, and other needs we might have. We were at a critical place with this needed repair. It wasn't as if we hadn't prayed before, but just before Brook and Landon moved in, we felt as if we were out of time. We prayed, "Lord, we are stepping out in faith. Please send the resources we need so that Landon and Brook will feel comfortable here."

As we prayed, we couldn't see how God would possibly do it, but we tried to believe He would supply our needs "according to the riches of His glory."

When Brook and Landon moved their belongings into the house, we knew we had to make the call. So, we called a plumbing company owned by a Christian man my husband had known for many years.

The plumbers arrived and crawled under the house to do their assessment. We held out hope that somehow we could apply a bandage to the situation that would buy us a little more time.

When at last one of the blue-uniformed plumbers emerged from under the house, his face bore a grim expression. "Has to all be replaced," he said. "Your cast iron pipes have a bunch of holes in them and they're full of material blocking the lines."

Our hearts sank. The repair money was nowhere in sight.

I gave my husband a desperate look.

"I'll make a call," he said. He telephoned the owner of the company, and asked if we could make monthly payments. The kind owner agreed, but I knew it would add a burden to an already taut budget.

Meanwhile, Brook came out of her bedroom into my office. She'd seen the plumbing truck in the driveway. "I know the people that own that company," she said. "I met them the same way I met you — at the restaurant."

I often went to write in the mornings at a restaurant where Brook had worked.

I nodded, but my chest felt tight as I pondered how we would manage the plumbing payments.

Brook went back to her bedroom and a few minutes later my husband appeared by my side. He had tears in his eyes. "The owner of the plumbing company called me back."

I held my breath. Had the owner reversed his decision about us making the monthly payments?

My husband continued, "He said he didn't know Brook and Landon had moved in with us. Because of our kindness to them, he's going to do the job for free."

My husband and I fell into each other's arms. Neither of us could have seen this coming. The only way the owner could have known is if Brook had said something to him.

I went to Brook and asked her what she'd done. "I didn't talk to him, but I did text his wife and tell her I saw their truck in the driveway and that we were living here temporarily, because we didn't have a place to stay."

I told her what these wonderful people had done for us.

The plumbers went to work, sawing and hammering pipes into place. The noise was deafening and went on for hours, but it didn't bother me. When one of the plumbers asked me to fill the washing machine and run it, I was afraid to leave the laundry room. But when it started emptying, there was no back flow. It ran smoothly.

As I listened to the water streaming down into the new pipes, I thought of all the things that came together to bring about this miraculous answer to prayer. We had invited Brook and Landon into our home by faith. She happened to be there when the plumbers came. She knew the owners of the plumbing company from her job at the restaurant, and she texted the wife. Then the wife had to talk to the husband about it. Much had to line up for us to get the call telling us the plumbing repair was free.

It wasn't even on our radar screen that something like that could happen. But it was definitely on God's. We had stepped out in faith, and God was right there to provide what we needed at exactly the right time.

Best of all for me, no more babysitting the washing machine.

22

Just Make a Sandwich

Tanja Dufrene

I asked if he wanted to take a lunch with him.

"No," came the predictable answer.

The answer was always, "No." It might be a couple of weeks or even a month before I would think to ask again. Typically, what triggered the conversation would be a few words he shared, that he just didn't feel good today. Then I would feel guilty, piling yet another layer on top of all that my mind was struggling to handle. His simple "No," brought me a breath of relief, although it was followed by a twinge of guilt and that voice within always whispering, *Just make a sandwich.*

Why did I not want to make a simple sandwich? Oh yeah, that's right. I was scrambling to get everything else done in my jam-packed days. I did not want to add another thing, no matter how simple or easy, no matter how little extra time it might require. My already mile-long To Do list was more than I could handle! Besides, why couldn't he make his own sandwich?

I already knew the answer to that. As much as he is fairly easy-going, he can be stubborn, too. He simply wouldn't. He would go without eating before packing a lunch or making a sandwich for himself.

I told myself I wanted my husband to know I loved and cared for him, but perhaps secretly I blamed him for my state of hurriedness and harriedness. Poor financial decisions on his part, and poor judgment calls on mine, had led us to heavy debt and a sense of daily despair. My constant pleas, likely turned nagging, fell on deaf ears. The more

I fought to turn things around, the more it appeared as though he withdrew. Over time, our conversations drifted to exchanges of necessary information. I felt as though we were roommates simply sharing space and bills as the burdens of life continued to drag us down.

With a growing bitterness within my soul, I quietly seethed with fury, acquiring a strong dislike for him. After all that had happened, I reasoned, I had every right to be displeased with him.

It was all too easy to blame him for our ills without reflecting on my own contribution to our unhappy state. Adding to all the pressure, I felt ignored and abandoned by the lack of communication. I justified my reasoning. *Shouldn't he be helping me more since I, too, work a full-time job? Why am I the one who has to just make a sandwich? Where is he while I am . . . .*

Finally, one day I decided to ignore the, "No,'" and followed the whispered voice telling me to *just make a sandwich.*

My husband has rarely been one to speak with insistence regarding what he wants. If I do this or if I don't do that, his words would never condemn me. But the Spirit kept prompting, *you know he needs to eat lunch, even if he will not ask you to make one for him. Just make a sandwich. He will probably eat it. And he will feel better at the end of the day.*

I wondered if he *would* eat it. Would he even remember to take it with him? To my surprise, he did.

So began our journey.

There were days I was so preoccupied with everything else that I completely forgot to pack him a lunch. He would graciously tell me not to worry about it, that he would find something. Yet all too often, he didn't. He would come home at the end of the day ravenous, ready for sustenance. Then I would make more of a conscious effort to remember. Pushing through my tiredness, I would prepare another sandwich.

Eventually I determined that preparing his lunch would not go undone. And I would resist the thoughts that barraged my mind about what I felt he was not doing for me. My job was to *just make a sandwich*, regardless.

At first, I made each sandwich from an obligatory attitude that sounded something like this in my mind: *Okay, Holy Spirit. You told me to do this, so I am. Here I am again, serving him! Doing more for him! And he is perfectly content to let me do more! When will he reciprocate?*

On and on the tirade went in my mind. I was not serving him because I wanted to, but because I knew disobeying the Holy Spirit would only lead to something worse than my already unhappy state. But in time, one sandwich after another, my heart began to soften. In those few moments of time it took to prepare his lunch, I began to pray. And the Spirit began to deal with my heart, revealing hardness, brokenness and to my surprise — unforgiveness.

My prayers started with complaints, begging for mercy and help so I could endure and somehow move beyond the silent prison in which I was suffering. But with the passing of time, I began to release my right to be angry. Conviction began to reveal a root of bitterness that had wrapped itself around me. As I repented and responded, my attitude and inner conversations became more bearable. One step at a time, I released thoughts and feelings of discontent. Rather than berate my husband in my mind for all of his shortcomings and failures, I began to search for qualities to praise. I began to look for opportunities to thank God for His provision through my husband, rather than relish what I saw as deficits and my right to be angry.

As my heart and attitude began to improve, my husband began to respond. The tension in the air gave way to a more pleasant tone. Eventually he seemed to be more attentive to me. I began to prepare each daily lunch with genuine passion and a heartfelt desire to serve him. I wanted to show him that he was a priority, regardless of our circumstances and how we got there.

Making his sandwich became an act of affection and love. Words did not have to be exchanged for this to become evident. Yet the words

I longed to exchange with him began to flow more easily and more naturally between us. And why?

I fully believe it was because I finally surrendered to the leading of the Holy Spirit to *just make a sandwich.*

Now I enjoy his affection, and he enjoys mine again. I treasure him more, and he treats me like a treasure. God knew it would require only a small act of service, a simple act of love to rekindle something that had grown cold between us. He knew what we needed and how to meet our need.

My part was to surrender, then surrender again, and again and again . . . one sandwich at a time. God began a work in me that changed me, reached through me and touched my husband. When I finally acted on it His simple little prompting to *just make a sandwich* transformed our relationship.

How many times might His promptings lead to greater joys if only we listen and act upon them? I wonder, is there someone for whom you simply need to *just make a sandwich?*

23

Patience Is a Virtue, So Hurry Up and . . .

Dr. Jayce O'Neal

Frustrations mounting, sweat-dripping, and steam coming out of my ears like a raging bull, I have again found myself at the end of my rope. What has me all bent out of shape, you might ask? Love life gone wrong? Nope. Problems at home? Nuh-uh. Money problems? Not really.

Then what?

I have again found myself irritated beyond belief, because of a stupid game called golf. Stupid being the operative word simply because the game is the problem and not my inability to play it . . . or so I tell myself over and over again. Most everyone knows that sports are often great tools to learn life lessons: being a team player, perseverance in the face of adversity, hard work paying off, etc.

However, this lesson I am currently facing is one I believe to be the toughest for many (including myself) to learn and live out in a practical manner in everyday life. I find that when I play golf, I become keenly aware that my patience is in short supply.

I have found that when an issue shows up in one part of my life, it can often be found in other places of my life as well. Sports can often act as a catalyst to reveal such things. Is there a fear of failure, an anger problem, or simply a lack of patience?

Patience. The very word can cause me to yawn, roll my eyes, or turn my attention to something else altogether. You see, I am a doer. I see something, I go after it. End of story. Being patient is not my cup of tea.

In fact, the thought of having to be patient seems to even increase my frustration. In football, if I get frustrated I just hit someone harder on the next play. In basketball, I can foul someone. In baseball, it's easier to hit the ball harder.

Then there's golf. In golf I really have no choice but to be patient.

When you get frustrated in golf and lose patience, you often land the ball in the sand trap, woods, or in my case, the window of that expensive house that just happened to get in the way of my ball.

I can often mistake patience and waiting on passivity, or I can see it as a convenient excuse for the lazy or the fearful. Yet I realize that this is not always the case.

I think if I were back in biblical times, I might have made different decisions than those I read about.

I think if I were Joshua instead of waiting for the seventh day, I might have instead knocked on the front door of Jericho after the first night. Perhaps if I were with Moses with the Red Sea in front of me and the Egyptians close behind, I might have jumped in the water and attempted to swim across.

This is not how I wish to be. I desire to be a man of faith . . . and a large part of that is to be a patient man. Being a patient man is not being passive or lazy, but rather being bold in confidence that God will do exactly what He promises to do. I want to be like Abraham who waited patiently and was rewarded for it. Hebrews 6:15 (NASB) tells us, *having patiently waited, he obtained the promise.*

When I think about it, it's nearly impossible to truly and honestly serve God faithfully and obediently without being a patient person who is willing to wait for the right thing at the right time. It is an odd thought to realize that my frustrations on the golf course can give me a glimpse into my relationship with God.

This being said, I can at least make strides in trusting the Lord and waiting for the right thing at the right time . . . even if I'm still paying home owners for windows broken because of my less-than-par golf game.

24

The Right Words at the Right Time

Peggy Ellis

We live with words: words that hurt, words that heal, words that confuse, words best left unsaid. In Philippians 3:13, Paul tells us to forget the past and look to the future. That's easier said than done, especially when hurtful words start early in life and continue for years.

It had been a long day and I started to wonder why had I signed up for my friend's workshop on writing memoirs. After all, my interest in writing was fiction, specifically cozy mysteries and Regency romances. Yet here I was taking a few notes and making surreptitious glances at my wristwatch.

Then, my ballpoint paused in midair. The instructor was saying, "Life has a way of changing our attitude about the past. In hindsight, we wonder why we allowed something, which was serious at the time, to continue affecting us. What changed our attitude toward something hurtful? And when?"

Attitude? What did that have to do with memories? Yet, her words struck a chord with me. I gripped the ballpoint. Not *what* changed my attitude. But *who*. Emma McKenzie!

The *when* had come many years after the hurtful words started.

The instructor's voice faded and remembered pain swept through me like a tsunami. My earliest memories buried in my subconscious sprang to life. It was 1941 again and I was a broken-hearted four-year-old keeping my face averted to avoid taunts. I was cross-eyed. The doctor told my parents I had to wait until I was six to have corrective surgery.

In the meantime, I learned to hide my tears when other little girls pointed their fingers and whispered. I grew accustomed to turning my head all the way to the left to see what was on that side. That brought more jeers and tears. Their words confused me. What difference did it make that my eyes were not exactly like theirs? Their eyes were not alike either. Some were blue, some were brown.

Sometime in the first week of October 1943 the day finally came for my surgery, I didn't care that I would miss six weeks of school. I didn't care that I had to lie flat on my back, my eyes bandaged, for nine days with a sandbag on each side of my head so I wouldn't jar the stitches loose. I didn't care that I would have to wear ugly wire-rimmed glasses. Nothing mattered because never again would anybody call me names like "Cock-Eyed" and I would have friends who let me join their games.

My contentment didn't last long. Soon I was called "Four Eyes" and the kids wouldn't play with me because they might break my glasses.

Reading became my consolation. *The Bobbsey Twins* took me to the seashore; the *Five Little Peppers* welcomed me into their games. In my mind, I played *Under the Lilacs* with Louisa Mae Alcott's *Eight Cousins*, and solved numerous mysteries with Nancy Drew. Nice people, all.

When I entered my teens, I started hearing things like, "Boys don't make passes at girls who wear glasses." That was true. Instead, they vied for the attention of my younger sister with her sky-blue eyes that didn't need glasses.

When I was sixteen God brought a special person into my life. During adolescence, I developed friendships with pen pals from several states; one of these was Emma McKenzie of Ontario, California.

Emma wrote the healing words that changed my life.

I don't recall where I found her name, but I praise God for it.

In introducing myself to Emma, I gave a description that included the statement, "I have the misfortune of wearing glasses." Her reply was prompt and unforgettable. "My glasses are my most prized possession because without them I can't see." Such wisdom from one sixteen-year-old to another. Would I have appreciated them at a younger age?

Probably not.

I can't count the number of times I've called forth Emma's healing words in times of distress, such as when people have told me I would be prettier without glasses. How hurtful people's careless words can be without their realizing it!

I also can't count the number of times I've made a point of telling little girls wearing glasses how pretty they are. This is a direct result of Emma's healing words. In hindsight, I realized God had prepared me to receive her words so I could encourage others.

I didn't change overnight. I remained a loner. The taunts continued, but I found it easier to ignore them as I repeated my mantra, "My glasses are my most prized possession because without them I can't see."

Through the years, I lost touch with most of my pen pals as life took us in different directions. However, letters to and from Emma continued.

If you aren't a letter writer, if you don't have distant friends whom you haven't seen in many years, you probably wonder if real friendship through mail is possible. I can tell you that it is. Emma and I congratulated each other on successes and commiserated over failures. We grieved together when family members went astray. We mourned together when our parents and siblings died. We encouraged each other when we felt no one else cared about the mundane details of our lives.

Our letters stopped only when her daughter told me Emma had gone home to heaven. That afternoon, I relived the few days I visited her in 1961. I again heard her musical voice when she called me in 1970 because she had misplaced my new address. I again watched her two children grow from babyhood, childhood, and adolescence into adulthood. My pain eased during those hours of chuckles and tears as I sat with my photo albums.

Our friendship began as pen pals, but I remember Emma McKenzie Lassley best as my dearest of friends. I wouldn't trade our friendship, physically distant though it was, for anything in this world. Someday, we'll meet where words don't hurt, so there's no need for healing words. We won't need our most prized possessions either.

Weeping may endure for a night,
But joy comes in the morning.

Psalm 30:5 NKJV

25

Healing Hurting Hearts

Diana C. Derringer

The telephone rang at 2 A.M. "This is the police department. We've picked up a mother and three children. The kids are in bad shape."

Once again I forced myself out of bed, looked over my well-worn list of foster families, and started calling. My goal: to find a family who could provide a safe, nurturing environment as well as keep the children together. Although on call twenty-four hours a day, seven days a week, I was thankful I could return to bed once I found that placement. The foster family's work had just begun.

During my almost thirty years as a social worker, physical, sexual, and emotional abuse or severe neglect colored my world. Drug abuse, mental illness, economic pressures, lack of support systems — a never-ending stream of dysfunction filled every day. Anger burned as I viewed bruises, burns, broken bones . . . a horrific mix of unimaginable scars inflicted by out-of-control adults. Sorrow followed as many children learned the defense, "I'm gonna hurt you before you hurt me." Their behavior spoke more loudly than words. Without intervention, they could easily follow their abusive parents' pattern.

I worked for a government agency. Nevertheless, that agency, along with nationally recognized trainers, shared in great detail and with eye-opening examples the biblical truth that in order to give love, we must first receive it. I daresay many of those specialists would have been shocked to realize how consistently their words matched those of Paul in Romans 15:7: *Accept one another, then, just as Christ accepted you.*

A frequently used expression matched those words: "We must parent the parents." Many of the adults in my caseload had never experienced genuine love and acceptance. They didn't know how to appropriately care for a child. Someone had to teach them. Words alone could not do the job. They had to see it and live it for themselves.

Yet I often faced the temptation to go through the motions without genuine love and respect. These families covered their brokenness with layer after layer of defensiveness, like onions. Finding a core of neediness under all that attitude demanded staggering amounts of patience and effort. Labeled as hopeless cases by more professionals than they could count, many had accepted that label and given up on themselves as well.

I wish I could say I consistently saw the potential God gave, or loved as God loves. In reality, I'm also a work in progress. But I did learn that when I allowed God to love through me — to change me, I increased the likelihood of lasting change in both parents and children. My training about the power of pain, illness, addiction, and negative thought and behavior patterns was never enough. I had to acknowledge everyone's inclination, including my own, to hurt others. By confessing my brokenness, I could more effectively minister to theirs.

Only when we acknowledge our personal imperfections can we point others to God's love, which heals the brokenness in us all.

My prayer, then as now: O God, work through me, love through me, heal through me.

26

Soaring with Eagles

Denise Valuk

A phone call in the middle of the night rarely brings good news. And quite frankly, I knew this one was coming.

"Denise," my aunt said gently, "it's your dad. I'm sorry. He's gone."

I didn't answer her. What could I say? Living with a suicidal father the past several years had taken a huge toll on me emotionally. Dad had already been hospitalized numerous times for suicidal behavior and had even taken a drug overdose the year prior and survived. This was no surprise.

"Do you want to know what happened?" she asked in a shaky voice.

"Sure." The only word I could mutter. Truth be told, I did not want to know. But Dad had been staying with his elderly parents by this point and I wanted to make sure they were all right.

The phone was silent, like my aunt was carefully choosing her next words. "He hanged himself out in the carport. Grandpa found him a little while ago."

At that point, I knew we had all been wrong. The entire family thought if we sent my dad back home to live with his parents, he would be safe. We never imagined he would kill himself at their house. How could any son do that his parents? Particularly ones who were in their eighties.

Dad's death was no surprise, yet I never considered the impact his action would have on me and my faith — the emotional pain, the isolation, the anger, or the questions I would face each day that followed.

I was horrified to tell my friends, especially my church family. This hesitancy was entirely on my part; they surrounded us with an atmosphere of love and care I will never forget. Yet, I could not help but feel I was a lesser person because of my father's suicide.

Then the guilt tumbled in, along with continued questioning of what else I could have done to prevent this tragedy. I sat up at night, thinking. What if I had shown my father more love? Was I not praying the right things during his illness? Did prayer even work? Where was God when this happened, and why had He let my father deteriorate to such a state that he took his own life?

I was empty, and worst of all, I felt like my faith had been lost. I could not find the words to comfort myself, my family, or anyone around me. I didn't pray.

Weeks passed. I woke up each morning with a feeling of emptiness, and then I would remember. Dad's gone. And he took his own life.

A close friend from church called me one day. "How are you feeling?" Wesley asked. "And I want the truth." He knew me too well. I was an expert at hiding my emotions.

"I'm numb. It's like I have lost all feeling," I admitted.

"Are you praying at all?" he asked in his usual persistent manner. If anyone could call me on my actions, it was Wesley.

I hesitated to answer. How would it sound if I said no, a seasoned Christian not turning to God in times of trouble?

"Well?" He wasn't going to let this go.

"No. I can't." I felt the slow trickle of a tear down my cheek. I didn't bother to wipe it off.

"Why not? Tell me what you are feeling," he insisted.

I sighed. I was exhausted from the endless nights awake, mindlessly flipping through the TV channels. "I don't have the energy. I can't form the words. I am just not strong enough."

"You need to find a way to pray, Denise. Even if it's only to ask why. It's all right to question God, but you have to turn to Him or else you won't start healing."

My friend was right. I knew he was, but it wasn't that simple.

Then a few days later, I received a card in the mail. I hurried into the house to open it. Many cards had arrived in the past month, and each one was a lifeline to me. Someone remembering my father. A friend or family member sharing my pain.

I pulled out the card and saw on the cover a familiar Bible verse from Isaiah 40:29-31: *He gives strength to the weary and increases the power of the weak. Even youths grow tired and weary, and young men stumble and fall; but those who hope in the LORD will renew their strength. They will soar on wings like eagles; they will run and not grow weary, they will walk and not grow faint.*

As I read this verse over and over again, I started to feel God's hand upon me. I still couldn't pray in the traditional sense, but I could say these words. I quickly memorized the verses and recited them during those long days and nights when I missed my dad so badly I felt like I couldn't breathe.

I had been spending my days at our family's business, helping my mother and brothers sort out the financial details of dad's death. One morning I walked into the small kitchen to make coffee, and I glanced at a framed picture of eagles with a Bible verse. It had been hanging there for years, but I had never really looked at it before.

Beneath the eagles on the picture was the verse from Isaiah I had been praying for weeks. Hanging by this picture were some framed photos of eagles my parents had taken at our family's lake house. The eagles were soaring above the trees, their majestic wings carrying them effortlessly through the sky. These pictures became regular stops for me during the day as I worked at my dad's business and tried to deal with my pain.

Shortly after I found this picture and verse on the wall, we attended a concert at our church. Our pastor had written a new song which used the words of Isaiah in the chorus. It was like divine appointment, as if the song had been written just for me.

I'll walk and not grow weary. Run and not be faint. I'll rise up like an eagle and fly away.

I listened to this song, letting the words wash over me like a gentle prayer. And I continued to pray the verse as I dealt with my father's suicide. Slowly, I changed the words. I asked God to give me strength, to increase my power, to help me run and not grow weary, to walk and not be faint.

Each day I felt God's healing strength flood my body and my mind. I meditated on these simple words, and began to form short prayers.

My heavenly Father knew traditional prayer would not come to me easily. Instead, He provided a verse, some pictures and a song. I know God sustained me with the images of eagles soaring high up in the sky.

27

Dad's Not Here

Rita Klundt

His hair more gray. His posture weak. His mind's slipping away.
He owns the home he shared with Mom. He still knows how to pray.
But Dad's not here.

He lives with other residents. His room has a nice view.
He sits for hours and contemplates, "Whatever did I do?"
But Dad's not here.

He strums his old guitar and sings his favorite gospel songs.
The chords rise up from memory when someone sings along.
But Dad's not here.

A lady, Betty Crocker type, prepares three daily meals.
Another makes his bed and cleans. Another gives him pills.
But Dad's not here.

Frustration seems to overcome the simplest of his tasks.
The question, "When can I go home?" he never fails to ask.
We try to entertain new thoughts; bring up good memories.
It's not our Dad who talks so mean.

They say, "It's the disease."
If Dad's not here, who is that man? He breaks our mother's heart?
She's lonely. She's committed that 'til death they'll never part.
But Dad's not here.

What can we do? There is no cure. The end is not in sight.
We'd battle with united front, but who or what to fight?
We look around, and yes, we see that we're not alone.
How many others bear this load as heavy as millstone?

Life does march on. We understand. We smile on top of sad.
'Til heaven calls to say he's home, we'll ask, "Where is our Dad?"
Dad's not here.

28

A Fragile Chain

Terri Elders

The trouble is, if you don't risk anything, you risk even more.
Erica Jong

I'd worn my half of the golden medal on a delicate gold chain for nearly seventeen years. On the morning we'd agreed to set our wedding date, Ken had shyly handed me a heart-shaped box containing two chains and two halves of a coin. When I'd fitted the two halves together, I read this verse from Genesis 31:49 (KJV), *The LORD watch between me and thee, when we are absent one from another.*

"It's a Mizpah," Ken had explained, as he'd fastened the fragile chain around my neck and I fastened the sturdier one around his. "The jeweler told me that the word *Mizpah* is Hebrew for watchtower, and it's a symbol of an agreement between two people to protect one another when separated by distance or even death."

I'd been impressed. I'd not known of my husband-to-be's fascination with mysticism, but he'd certainly believed in magic. Why, Harry Houdini had been his personal hero, and Ken frequently showed me card and coin tricks he'd learned from magician buddies.

Then one evening last autumn I stepped out of my bedtime shower and grabbed a towel. The jagged inner edge of my Mizpah charm snagged on a few terrycloth threads. I gave a little tug, and to my horror the chain snapped in two and clattered to the floor, Mizpah flying free.

Blinking back tears, I bent down and scooped up the pieces from the bathroom floor. Even though a jeweler had warned me that the chain was wearing thin, I had not considered putting it away and wearing it only on special occasions. Since Ken had given me the gift, I'd removed it only when I'd undergone surgery.

After Ken had died, I'd removed my wedding ring, having no problem with the world knowing that I was no longer a married woman. But I felt differently about my Mizpah. By continuing to wear it, I'd sensed Ken's spirit watching out for me. Now, without that dainty chain around my neck, I suddenly felt alone.

"I'll just buy another chain," I assured myself, climbing into bed. As I drifted into sleep, the number seven began to dance into my dreams. When I awakened the next morning, my fingers flew to my throat. I patted my bare neck.

Why had my dream been filled with a parade of sevens? I puzzled for a few moments and then realized that seven years had elapsed since Ken died. Coincidentally, I'm nearing the close of my seventh decade. That morning, it seemed that Ken was telling me I had mourned long enough. It was time to move on with my life.

"Seven is supposed to be a holy number," I remembered. Seven is significant. There are seven days in a week. Seven colors of the rainbow. Seven wonders of the ancient world. Seven notes on a musical scale. Seven seas and seven continents. Even the movie, *Seven Brides for Seven Brothers.* Seven appears over seven hundred times in the Bible. It connotes concepts such as completion and perfection, exoneration and healing, and the fulfillment of promises and oaths. Maybe seven years of wearing the Mizpah was sufficient in showing my loyalty.

I glanced at the curio cabinet in the corner that displays my collection of crystal unicorns. Since girlhood I've been beguiled by the beauty of these graceful mythical beasts. I'm always gladdened when on holidays I open unicorn cards from friends. For decades I've fished in my handbag for my unicorn keychain. I've even traveled to Paris and to New York City to pay homage to the unicorn tapestry collections at their medieval museums, the Cluny and the Cloisters.

Legend has it that the unicorn, a master of transformation, bestows on mortals the power to believe that anything is possible. Could a unicorn charm give me a new lease on life, a new beginning? Would it be all right for me, at my mature age, to wish for someone new to share my dreams? I imagined Ken somewhere far away nodding reassuringly.

I knew, as well, that the collective noun for unicorns is "blessing." I certainly could use a blessing. So I searched online and ordered a new gold chain and a gold unicorn chain.

Then, still at the computer, I took a deep breath, and located an online dating site. After all, I'd met Ken through one all those years ago. I don't believe that lightning can't strike twice. Still, it had been a long time since anyone held my hand at a concert or a movie, or leaned over to kiss me. Would I even know how to respond, I wondered, as I began to fill out an application. Would I know what to do?

"Sure, it's a risk," I reminded myself, "but what will I gain if I don't try?" Even if I didn't meet anybody who was on my wavelength, at least I'd have tried.

I finished answering the final questions on the profile questionnaire and clicked on "send."

It didn't happen right away. But finally, about seven months later I found a possible match, a man who called himself "friendly author." I dashed off a note, describing myself as a writer as well. He answered, telling me the title of his book.

As we continued to correspond, we began to marvel at our similarities. We're the same age. We went to rival high schools at the same time in the same city. We're alums of the same university. We like the same authors, the same music, the same sports.

There were at least seven synchronicities. Maybe seven hundred would be a closer estimate.

We met in person and discovered even more common and uncommon interests. I told him about my dream of the parade of sevens. He laughed. I think he knew before I did that he was the blessing I had wished for.

Yes, we held hands at the movies. And when he finally kissed me, I knew what to do.

"We seem to be riding the same wavelength of the universe," he recently said.

I agree.

I'm enchanted. Blessed. Charmed. A life confirmed by a Parade of Sevens.

29

Dishing Up Love

Barbie Porter

A sigh of satisfaction blew through my lips as I carefully placed the cup, wrapped in newspaper, atop the other dishes in the cardboard box.

Hands on hips, I stood there remembering the day I had received the dishes. They were a gift from a co-worker's mom, whom I had never met, as I was stepping into a new chapter of my broken life as a single mom. To this very day we have never met, yet I couldn't help but think she might be pleased with what I was about to do with the dishes.

A smile stretched across my face as the Sharpie and I wrote, "To Pat" punctuated with a little heart on one of the box flaps.

Two days earlier I had made my first visit to the home of my friend, Pat. While giving me a tour of her charming farmhouse, she proudly showed me the many pieces of her glassware collections scattered throughout the rooms. They were eclectic and beautiful. Last, she led me to her kitchen where she pulled out her four favorite pieces of Homer Laughlin. She knew I had some like them since we had often swapped stories of our hunt for the illusive dishes.

While holding her only plate in her hand, Pat slipped into reminisce mode, sharing about how her grandmother had had dishes just like these and the wonderful meals she used to serve on them. She summed it all up by saying, "One day I'm going to have a complete set." We both smiled then headed out the door to work on a mission project.

My set of Homer Laughlin was far from complete, just a few plates, some saucers, three cups, one bowl, two little platters, and a sugar bowl. But oh, how I loved the delicate little pink and blue rose clusters ribboned in warm burgundy in the now-crackled white China encircled by a dainty gold band. Coupled with the unique way in which they were given to me, they seemed to make every meal more homey, more sweet. That's why I too had longed for a complete set.

The honking car horn caused me to grab the box of glassware and place it on the loveseat before leaving with Pat to have lunch.

After lunch, we went straight to my kitchen to work on the mission task at hand.

Pleased with our completed project, with a cuppa in hand, we settled in the living room. Pat sat next to the box, just as I hoped she would.

"That is for you," I said, pointing to the box.

Reaching toward the box Pat said, "Is it the lamp globe you told me about?"

I didn't respond, but watched as she opened the box and unwrapped the first piece.

"What?" she exclaimed. "Barbie, you didn't."

I smiled.

"They're just like the ones Grandma used to use, you know. Did you know my Grandma raised me?"

I didn't know that, but the look on her face told of a deeper, sweeter, yet broken story. Tears filled her eyes as she expressed what this gift meant to her.

A warmth filled my heart as I carried the box out to her car and watched her drive away. I thought, *This is probably how that lady felt when she gave those dishes to me.*

A few days later, I received word from Pat that our mission director from Haiti was her guest and I was invited to join them for a working breakfast at her house.

Greeted by the small work team, and enticing smells of a homecooked meal, I was quickly escorted to the kitchen. The table was a country breakfast dream, loaded with biscuits and gravy, eggs and bacon, muffins and rolls, coffee, tea, and juice. But, of course, the main attraction was the beloved tableware — a sweet mixture of shared treasures.

A few months passed and as the holiday season approached, Pat told me of her plans to bring her mother home from the nursing home for Thanksgiving dinner. She knew it would be a challenge since her mother was a victim of Alzheimer's mixed with a severe case of Sundowners, which brought increased confusion and stress at the close of the day. But Pat's heart wanted her mother there.

A few days later I received a call.

"Barbie, I just gotta tell you what happened," Pat said before I could say a word.

"You know how Mom is," she said. "We brought her home. She didn't even recognize me when we picked her up, and she didn't recognize our house, but when she stepped into the kitchen and saw the dishes . . . her eyes lit up. Then she said, 'Oh, look . . . Mother's crackled dishes.'"

Pat paused for a moment, then continued. "After that, she was as calm as could be. We ate dinner and enjoyed our entire visit, even the trip back to the nursing home was pleasant."

That was Pat's mother's final visit to her house.

Sure, they're only dishes.

But . . . sometimes I wonder. Just how much love can one crackled dish hold?

30

Fix It

Christina Sinisi

The first time I fell in love at first sight wasn't with my husband, even though he's the love of my life and we will soon celebrate our thirty-fourth wedding anniversary.

No, the first time was when, after a long labor and an unexpected Cesarean section, I held my son. It was late at night. My husband had gone home for some needed rest and the usually-bustling hospital corridors were hushed. When a nurse gave me my son to hold, and left me alone with the little miracle, time and space narrowed down to the cocoon of my arms and just the two of us.

His blue eyes met mine — don't tell me newborns can't see that well — and I knew I was totally smitten.

Two, almost three years later, months of colic, teething, and the biting stage behind us, we were in the backyard of our first house. The yard had a cement patio and scrubby grass dotted with red-ant hills. Scott was all boy and, yes, I'm his mother, but I'm not exaggerating when I say he was brilliant. He knew all the dinosaur names and whether each one was a plant eater or a meat eater. We had lengthy discussions about what caused their mass extinction — the meteor crashed and caused fires and then the plant eaters didn't have any food. Since the plant eaters were all gone, then the meat eaters didn't have any food.

His vocabulary increased every day.

He was brimming over with energy — running around the yard, climbing up and down his little plastic slide. He had one of those little orange plastic cars that he bumped over the cement and into the grass, undeterred by tree roots and cracked concrete.

When he stepped in a red ant pile, I came running. I brushed the ants off his legs and ripped of his shoes and socks. I fixed it. When he tripped and hit the side of our coffee table, an emergency room visit later, I fixed it. When he was hungry or thirsty or in need of being held, I fixed it.

But then he accidently stomped on a cricket and held out its lifeless body. "Fix it," he demanded.

Of course, I couldn't.

That was a small broken moment, but I've never forgotten it.

It wasn't the first time, and it certainly hasn't been the last, but I remember that minute, those sheer seconds when I had to tell my child that I couldn't fix it. The cricket was dead. I couldn't bring it back to life.

There was a glimmer of the first time my child realized that sometimes actions have consequences and those can't be fixed, either. There was a realization that Mama wasn't all-powerful and she could disappoint him. In such moments, I wasn't enough.

None of us is all-powerful. Bad things will happen in our lives, some due to our choices and thoughtlessness; some completely out of our control.

Realizing these things can hurt, but it would hurt even more to *not* realize our need to depend on the One who is enough. We all, including me and my son, need to know that only Christ is enough, that only God is all-powerful.

And, whatever the problem, when the time is right, He will fix it.

31

Intercession

Steve Carter

The sudden gust from the eighteen-wheeler and the noise of the massive engine blowing by shook me to the core, but my fright was short-lived. A quick, friendly blast from the truck's air horn signaled approval of the large American flag flying from my trike.

This late night encouragement, along with cheering, friendly waves, and a television interview, all since I had started in International Falls, Minnesota, supported my reason for peddling from "Canada to Key West, Florida."

I initially planned the trip for the sake of scenery and to "test my mettle" physically and mentally. However, in light of the lack of respect being shown nationwide for our flag, I decided to fly a larger one as a statement of thanks to our military veterans and to display my fierce patriotism.

Now, after twelve hours of peddling on my recumbent trike, I found myself drifting into traffic because I could no longer focus. In the wake of the near miss, I immediately pulled over. This close encounter made it obvious I had put myself in extreme danger. After setting the hand brakes, I stumbled upright, stepped over the wheels, and reviewed the events leading to my predicament.

Riding through southern Missouri had proven much more physically and mentally taxing than I had anticipated. This section of my "Canada to Key West Ride" blessed me abundantly while simultaneously exposing me to a depth of misery I had never before experienced. Many long days peddling, followed by inadequate rest in seedy motels, had caught up with me. Poor nutrition, consisting of mostly peanut butter, crackers, and sports drinks, was taking a toll on my endurance, thus slowing my attempt at dodging the day's heat.

Immediately after a pre-dawn start, my legs still tired, problems had set in with the endless, steep hills. Although my knees were supported by braces, my hands had soon beguan to cramp from constant gear changing and braking. After nearly stalling when I ran out of gears, I'd anticipated a flat tire. Finally, I had set the brakes, climbed off the trike, stumbled around, and poked the tires. I had been happy that I didn't have to fix a flat, but my spirits had sagged a little because my legs were already all but exhausted.

Morning had passed quickly before I reached the southbound four-lane road that pointed me toward Memphis. Although I was markedly happier with my own lane to ride in, the improvement came at a price. Instead of small-town traffic and confusing road signs, very large, fast-moving trucks now kept me company. Motels and places to buy nutrition had become increasingly scarce . . . which could lead to low blood sugar and dehydration.

Normally, when riding over terrain like what graced this part of Missouri, I restricted my mileage to under eighty miles a day. Unfortunately, the state's rural countryside lacked ample lodging and convenience stores. Now, with darkness fast approaching, my supplies a fading memory, aching legs all but dead, and over thirty miles between me and the next motel, I felt an unfamiliar dread.

I unclipped my shoes from the pedals and struggled to stand. In an effort to regain circulation to my lower extremities, I stumbled around, wondering if falling into the road or a ditch would win out.

Although I normally relied on my own strength during times of duress, tonight I realized from experience gleaned while peddling twice across the country that I was in serious trouble.

My recumbent trike consists of a seat the size of a lawn chair, three wheels to keep me from falling over, and handle bars for steering. Having napped on it numerous times, I knew it would be more comfortable than sleeping in a ditch. Scanning the surrounding underbrush and trees, I began to plan a night sleeping on my trike.

That's when I suddenly felt God thump me on the head.

"Call the church."

I pulled my phone out and hit speed dial.

Brother Reggie, who was on call that night, answered. As soon as I heard his voice, I knew everything was going to be all right because that man is a prayer warrior of the highest order. I told him about my dire straits, which grabbed his attention. Reggie did not just say "I'll pray for you," and go back to watching television like many would have. This man of God went to work immediately praying an intercessory prayer on my behalf. Afterwards, I knew God had answered our plea.

Strength and spirit renewed, I thanked him repeatedly.

He responded, "When I heard the ring, I almost didn't answer, but God told me to."

I assured him we would talk again soon and I headed south, leaning into the remaining three hours of hills.

After a mile or two, I spotted the lights of a convenience store glowing in the darkness about a half mile off the highway. I'm convinced God's timing had a hand in my seeing that place; I probably would have missed it in the daylight due to concealing trees.

While stocking up I, must have been a pitiful sight because several people offered me food and shelter. But with rain in the next day's forecast, I acknowledged their courtesy and got back on the road.

My legs' strength was renewed following Reggie's prayer, and I steadily ground out the remaining miles into Poplar Bluff, Missouri. The miles however were not, by any stretch of the imagination, easy. Large trucks roared past me on the fog-shrouded highway. Confusing road signs and an almost-dead phone battery made navigation even more difficult. But just before midnight, after one-hundred thirteen miles, I rolled into the lobby of the motel I had booked.

Following a much-needed shower, I gave thought to how the day had given me a better understanding of intercessory prayer. For nearly twenty-five years had I suffered with Meniere's syndrome, an inner-ear disease. Despite numerous prayers for healing, I'd endured multiple surgeries, trips to emergency rooms, and vertigo-induced bicycle crashes, all of which God could have prevented but didn't. These struggles challenged my faith as I participated in several ministries and strived to be a good father and husband.

Enduring sickness for so much of my life had left me skeptical about the effectiveness of intercessory prayer. However, after experiencing the miracle of renewed leg strength and the unexpected nutrition I was able to purchase, I gained great insight into the wisdom of following the guidance of the Holy Spirit.

Thankfully, I had obeyed God's prompting and called Reggie for help. Answering the phone displayed Reggie's servant's heart, which prompted a mighty, heartfelt prayer. As a result, God heard our prayer and answered, giving me renewed physical and mental strength, as well as nourishment for my body.

I'll never know for certain what would have been the cost of ignoring God's instructions to call the church that miserable evening in Missouri. My fate without Reggie being guided to answer the phone is anybody's guess. However, I'm convinced without our obedience and Reggie's powerful prayer, my time on earth could well have ended on that dark hostile road in the Missouri hills.

32

When We Ask God to Move

Diana Leagh Matthews

All day I'd had a heavy spirit that I'd been unable to shake. I tried praying, but the words did not come. I'd only been at this place of employment for nine months. In that time I'd gone from loving my job to detesting being there. I had been praying for months about what to do and if this was really where God wanted me.

It was nothing unusual to have a heavy heart while at work, but today it was a different feeling. Even when I'd taught our Bible study, the darkness only lifted briefly, returning with a stronger force than before.

"The executive director wants to see you," my co-worker said a short time later. I knew that wasn't good news. I attempted to pray on the short walk to her office, but again the words would not come.

As I walked into the office and took in the three faces waiting for me, I realized my intuition had been correct. Something was definitely wrong.

I took the seat indicated and listened. As words were repeated that I'd confided to a fellow co-worker, my heart began to sink. She was a person I thought was a friend. However, she had betrayed my confidence and at times took a portion of my words out of context.

I thought back to a few days earlier when I'd confided in her about a friendship I had with a resident's family member. A voice had whispered into my spirit at that moment to stop talking, yet I continued expressing my feelings.

Nothing inappropriate happened with the person I was confiding about, my feelings had just changed in the last month to being more personal. I had not shared that with the man, or anyone else. I'd resolved never to tell him. Yet, I knew it was clear in how I reacted to him that I could care for him in a deeper way.

These feelings were not without reservations. He had been single for a long time, was considerably older than I, our personalities were as different as oil and water, and I knew he was not open to a relationship. He made it clear to everyone that he was a lifelong confirmed bachelor. I knew a relationship beyond friendship was improbable.

However, I had related my feelings to the woman I considered a friend, as conversation about him being the kind of man I could really care for. The last thing I ever wanted him to know was that I could be serious about someone like him.

Now, he had been made aware of my emotional attachment, enhanced by the woman I thought was a friend. Not only had she betrayed me, but he had complained to management without confronting me. In those moments I saw a side of him I had not known existed and did not particularly admire. I could not understand why he would feel upset instead of complimented.

Three weeks earlier, when I realized deeper feelings had evolved, I had prayed, "Lord, if he is not the man for me, please make it clear."

I had already suffered so much heartache. I did not want my heart broken again. After two bad and abusive relationships, I knew I could not relive another similar situation.

I listened to the executive director speak, sensing the words that were coming before they were spoken. I'd wondered how God would answer my prayer, but it definitely wasn't this way.

I had been given a glimpse of a man who was upset that someone could care for him. As the primary caregiver for his parents, he was an upset client. We all know the old adage: The customer — or in this instance the client — is always right.

As I was let go from my job, I prayed, "Lord, I didn't expect this and I don't know what to do, but I forgive him." I was surprised at how easy it was to forgive this man who had a piece of my caring heart . . . especially in the face of abject rejection and humiliation.

As I drove off the premises, I was shaken and at a loss. I had no idea where to go or what I was going to do. I went to a nearby church, where my ancestors were buried, and stayed the four hours until dusk as I prayed and cried.

I was in shock. I tried bargaining with God, wondering if a mistake had been made. "They will call tomorrow and tell me there was a mistake and I'm not fired from my job, after all," I told myself that night.

But one day passed. Then two. Then three. I spoke with a trusted friend, but could not share my humiliation with anyone else.

For the remainder of the week, I did the only thing I knew to do. I fasted, prayed and walked to help my stress level. I struggled with shock and bargaining, which led to anger. "Why?" I cried out. I longed to throttle that man, while at the same time I still cared for him.

I pulled out a notepad and wrote letters that expressed my feelings. After I finished, I burned the letters to prevent me from ever mailing them. Just writing made me feel better.

However, as I walked and prayed I was surprised by my actions. I began to earnestly pray for the man. I prayed his walk with our Lord would grow stronger and stronger. I prayed that one day I would see him in heaven and be able to tell him I forgave him for that public display and rejection. I prayed God would melt the hardness the man had built around his heart. I prayed for God to restore his relationship with his siblings, from whom he'd been estranged for years.

The following months were difficult, but God provided a job to tide me over while I continued searching for work in my field. Then a door opened for a much better position than the one from which I'd been fired. This was a position like I had wanted at my last place of employment, but for which the executive director had refused to consider me.

Working through the pain of betrayal took another year, but it slowly began to subside. I discovered that while it was easy to forgive the man who betrayed me in such a public way, it was more difficult to forgive the person I'd confided in, the executive director, and others who were indirectly involved. Again, I had to pray earnestly and intentionally forgive them.

In Jeremiah 29:11, God tells us that He knows the plans He has for us. They are plans to prosper us and not to harm us, but to give us hope and a future.

God heard my prayers and knew my concerns and unhappiness. He answered my prayers, although not the way I envisioned them being answered. Often, His answers are not what we asked for, but as the Bible tells us His ways are not our ways. God remained faithful to me during this trial and allowed all the pieces to fall into place.

Today, I am in a much better place and much happier. Looking back, I see how God used that experience as a stepping stone to move me where He needed me, professionally and emotionally.

When we ask God to move, He will move in His timing and His way. He just asks that we remain faithful to Him.

33

Making Turtles

Diana C. Derringer

think we need to make some turtles."

We had not seen Anne for several years. She had completed her education, married, and moved to another town. She enjoyed a successful teaching career and was expecting her first child. Although as beautiful and outgoing as always, grief overwhelmed her.

Standing with her mother and sister, she accepted condolences from friends and family during visitation at a local funeral home. Her father had suffered a sudden, massive heart attack. He died within moments. The physical and emotional strain left her drained. Yet, when my husband and I drew near, she smiled through her tears. While we hugged and held to one another, she'd whispered her desire.

Fun Times

We'd created those wonderful gooey, caramel-filled, chocolate-covered candies when she and her sister were in elementary school. My turtle molds had been relegated to a shelf of seldom- or never-used items soon after. However, with those few words, floods of memories returned.

Anne and Val's father and my husband had worked together, and our friendship grew through shared family recreation. We'd invited the girls to stay with us several times, and one of our favorite activities was working in the kitchen, especially making turtles. Although probably the least nutritious of our creations, what fun it was to pop them from their molds and hear the girls exclaim, "We made them all by ourselves!" Vitally important decisions followed: "Whose turtle do you think looks best?" "Should we eat the head or body first?"

In the process we made messes, giggled, talked, and endured endless teasing from my husband. While busy putting her turtles together, Anne remained at his mercy. Nevertheless, she shot back verbal retorts and became a master at creative faces.

I can't recall spending a great deal of time discussing deep theological issues. We said our usual prayer of thanks before eating. We read the Bible and prayed together at night. We discussed school and other activities. Most of the time we simply enjoyed one another's company.

Hard Times

Little did we realize how God would use those fun-filled days to help us through one of the hardest times of our lives.

Through our grief, we gained several insights.

- **Recognize the uniqueness of every situation.** We don't have a mold that fits all. Therefore, we need to respect each person and family for where they are and what they need.
- **Presence trumps platitudes.** Sometimes we need no words. Instead we should quietly share the moment or offer a clasped hand or hug.
- **Remember special times together.** Making turtles helped our situation. Although remembering, laughing, and holding did not remove the grief, they did make our grief more manageable. Romans 12:15 (HCSB) tells us to *rejoice with those who rejoice; weep with those who weep.*
- **Admit limitations.** Sometimes we must simply say, "I don't know why this is happening, but I want you to know that I will be here for you through it all."
- **Hold fast to faith.** Pray. Embrace God's comfort and presence. Experience and share God's agape love.
- **Look for the good that can come from every difficulty.** As Paul wrote in Romans 8:28 (HCSB), *We know that all things work together for the good of those who love God: those who are called according to His purpose.*

- **God desires time with us.** We don't have to use lofty theological language or pray only when our hearts fill with sorrow. God offers to share our daily joys and provide for our ongoing growth. Then when life's inevitable difficulties arise, that relationship, strong and vital, provides an unlimited source of comfort.

Anne's family and ours loved and supported one another. In a far greater way, God loves and supports each of us.

34

God's Divine Peace

Alice Klies

I turned my eyes away from my doctor's smiling face as he began the examination. I hated the yearly visit to my gynecologist. Now, certain that menopause fogged my brain, nothing could have prepared me for the words slipping quietly out of my doctor's mouth.

"Alice, did you know you are about three months pregnant?"

I almost stood in the stirrups holding my feet. Had I heard him right?

"What? You've got to be kidding. Impossible. I'm 44 years old!"

I felt bile creep into the back of my throat. Before another strangled word sprang from my lips, my doctor gently laid his hand on my shoulder.

"I'm not kidding Alice. You're pregnant. Because of your age we'll need to get you into a specialist and do some tests, but you should be fine."

I left the doctor's office on legs that wobbled all the way to my car. Once I was in the front seat, my head fell forward onto the steering wheel. I turned my head to look up toward the blue sky. Tears made their way down my face. "Oh God. Is this some kind of a joke?"

My husband, of only eight months, would be home from work, probably watching the five-o'clock news. I slipped through the front door. "Hi honey," I said. "How was your day?"

Ray looked up. "Great." He patted the couch seat. "Come join me."

I sat, my head spinning. *I'm pregnant.*

I snuggled close to Ray. In a hushed whisper I said, "Uh, I have something to tell you. I went to the doctor today and he told me I'm pregnant."

Ray pulled away from me for just a second before he nearly pulled me off the couch. "Really?" His eyes misted before his arms enveloped me. "This is great news. Wow! I can't believe it. Wow! We're going to have a baby!"

Three months later, I was in our local hospital emergency room. My labor had began suddenly. I knew the danger of delivering our baby at twenty-seven weeks' gestation and it scared me beyond reason. When it became evident our baby might arrive early, the local hospital transferred me to a hospital specializing in preemie births.

Riding in an ambulance is downright scary!

I lay on my side, in labor, for three days. Our baby's feet inched toward the birth canal first. The umbilical cord wrapped around a foot gave our doctor grave concern for my safety as well as our baby's. He came into the labor room to tell us, "If we can get corticosteroids in you for forty-eight hours, your baby's lungs might have a better chance to mature."

Use of steroids reduces by half the incidence of hyaline membrane disease. This occurs when the tiny air sacs collapse and stick together with every breath because of the lack of a substance known as surfactant, which provides surface tension in the lungs' air sacs.

We agreed to the procedure. Two days later, my situation became critical. If a C-Section wasn't performed immediately, the already-strained water sac might break, which could put both our baby and me in jeopardy. Doctor's explained our early term baby might not survive. I thought, *How can I survive this?*

The anesthesiologist numbed me from the waist down. Even though I stayed awake, the whole scene felt surreal. I examined the faces surrounding me. I saw anxious eyes and furrowed foreheads above the white masks that doctors and nurses wore. Two Neonatal specialists stood at my feet. Off to my left, against a wall, stood two nurses who busily attended to an incubator that had wires and machines attached to it. Within minutes, I became aware that a skilled hand had neatly drawn an incision across my belly. I felt Ray's hand tighten on my shoulder as he kissed my forehead and whispered, "It's okay Alice, Jesus is right here with us."

One of the doctors almost shouted, "We have a baby girl. One pound, nine ounces." I lifted my head in an effort to see her but she had already been handed off to one of the nurses, placed in the incubator and whisked out the door.

When a nurse wheeled me to the Neonatal Intensive Care Unit to see our baby for the first time, my stomach churned. My brokenness felt beyond fixing. Our baby's eleven-inch torso glowed under phototherapy lights to correct her jaundiced color. Wires and tubes seemed to grow out of her arms, chest and feet. A tiny blindfold covered her eyes. Her transparent skin made her blue veins stand out like lines on a road map.

As we asked questions about the wires and machines. A nurse explained that preemies are born with little subcutaneous fat, the thermal layer directly under the skin which controls the baby's temperature. "Since a preemie's nervous system is not developed, your baby can't shiver or sweat. The sensor attached to her ensures us that she is neither too hot nor too cold. If we don't monitor this, she might burn calories she can't afford to lose."

An alarm attached to her chest told them when our baby forgot to breathe. If undetected, her heart rate could slow down. This is called bradycardia, and can cause sudden death.

None of this information made me feel better. I wanted to touch her, hold her to my chest. I wanted to protect her. Instead, all I could do was listen, sit still, and sob.

In the weeks that followed, a choice I had made many years earlier began to haunt me. *Am I being punished? Am I being brought to my knees with brokenness for a past sin, when I made one of the most devastating choices ever?*

My new relationship with Christ kept me on bended knee. I believed I'd been forgiven for an abortion I'd had during an abusive earlier marriage. Yet, after seeing our tiny baby, I struggled with the impending trials ahead and this past sin. Maybe God had given me a second chance by gifting this baby to us. Maybe He wanted me to understand how precious and fragile life is. Maybe He needed me to treasure this life He gave me at age forty-four.

Yes, God had forgiven me, but maybe I needed a constant nudge to remember my disobedience. Was this my chance to right a wrong? Was He making it a little harder for me so I had to put all my trust in Him to bring us through this trial?

Soon, our baby flourished beyond any of our expectations. After she spent nearly three months in intensive care, we took her home. She weighed three pounds fourteen ounces. I had always thought a baby had to weigh five pounds in order to leave a hospital but our pediatrician said, "She is eating, sleeping and going to the bathroom. She is ready."

The hospital offered a program designed for mothers with preemies. I took the opportunity to spend a night at the hospital in a room alone with our baby before we took her home.

It was a comfort to know that her nurse, who had delivered her, would be close by. Along with several diapers and formula, she gave me a hug and closed the door. I stared at my sleeping baby. Only minutes passed before the alarm on her heart monitor blared. Although I'd heard it many times, I couldn't shake the feeling of dread. I reached over the opening in the incubator and gently massaged her tiny chest to help her breathe.

I gingerly reached into the side of her diaper, so as to not wake her, to see if she needed to be changed. She started to whimper. I knew she might be hungry so I fumbled with her formula. Her cry became more intense. I giggled because I remembered a time when all she could do was squeak. She now had lungs that belted out her impatience for a bottle like a lion's roar. Her mouth grabbed on to the nipple with a force that surprised me. This was repeated every two hours.

I opened a drawer on the nightstand next to my bed, picked up a Bible and thumbed through the pages. It slipped out of my hands and fell open on the floor. When I bent over to pick it up, a shiver ran down my spine. I thought someone had come into the room. I continued to glance about the room before I retrieved the Bible from the floor. I couldn't shake the feeling someone was in the room with me.

Since I'd never read a Bible before, I started to read the scripture in front of me. *Put off your old self, which belongs to your former manner of life and is corrupt through deceitful desires and . . . be renewed in the spirit of your mind and put on the new self, created after the likeness of God in true righteousness and holiness* (Ephesians 4:22-24 ESV).

Torrents of tears ran down my face. I read the passage over and over. I thought about the life I had ended and reflected on the person I used to be. I remembered my humble confession. Once again, I felt a presence, only this time, warmth spread across my chest. Was I getting sick?

I flipped pages only to land on, *I rejoice . . . because you were grieved into repenting, for you felt a godly grief, so that you suffered no loss through us. For godly grief produces a repentance that leads to salvation without regret, whereas worldly grief produces death. For see what earnestness this godly grief has produced in you, but also what eagerness to clear yourselves, what indignation, what fear, what longing, what zeal, what punishment! At every point you have proved yourselves innocent in the matter* (2 Corinthians 7:8-11).

My limbs trembled. My heart raced. I whispered, "Are you here Jesus?" When I glanced at my sleeping baby, light from the head of my bed shone on her face. It illuminated her peaceful slumber. I prayed out loud, "Okay Jesus, I hear you. I've given you a lot of lip service and not much commitment."

I stayed awake all night. The more I read, the more proof the Bible fed me that I shouldn't try so hard to be self-sufficient or over confident without direction from my Savior.

I don't think it is a fluke I opened a drawer in the hospital to discover a book that changed my life. I believe Jesus orchestrated everything that occurred. I believe His presence in my room that night opened my eyes. I finally understood. I am a forgiven child of His. I can witness, through my own experience, how belief in Jesus does offer us peace and eternal salvation no matter what trials we face in our lifetime.

Our tiny preemie grew up to be a beautiful young woman and follower of Christ. I continue to grow in my faith by devouring every piece of scripture in my Bible. Since that night in the hospital, whenever I pray and ask for forgiveness, I get a fluttering up my spine. It only last seconds. I always feel a deep sense of peace. I can only survive with His help!

35

Shattered

Jean Matthew Hall

Each New Year's Day I try to retreat and spend that day conversing with God. Each year I do less talking and more listening, it seems. God always gives me a theme or emphasis for the coming year — an area of my life that He will be working on that year. During my 2015 retreat the Holy Spirit impressed on me to pray for personal brokenness, to seek brokenness and to anticipate its coming.

That's not an easy thing to experience.

Through the year various people and events drove me to my knees, then to my face on the floor. I spent much time in tearful prayer in the solitude of my office. After each event I would think, *Is this it, Lord? Surely my life can't get more painful. Surely I've reached the point of being broken and poured out. Right, God?*

But it wasn't until autumn that God drove the final nail into my heart — the nail that broke my heart into tiny shards.

My daughter had been married for twelve years. She and her husband have four beautiful children. They are precious to me. Because of their parents' work schedules, the children spent almost as much time with me as with their parents. In essence I became a third parent.

In mid-September my daughter packed up her children and her things and left her husband. It caught me totally by surprise. On the surface they seemed happy. I was consumed with other problems in my life, and hadn't seen their problems.

I struggled to understand her decision. I tried talking to each of them, interceding on behalf of their family. She wouldn't give me any details that would help me understand better, make me feel better. I tried. But I couldn't come to peace with their separation. I tried to convince her that their family was worth fighting for. But she was adamant that separation and divorce were the only acceptable answer.

I prayed for understanding. I grieved. I moaned and groaned at the Lord's feet. But peace eluded me. It was one of the most painful events of my life. I'm sure it was even more painful for them.

A month or two after my daughter left her husband I was at the point of total despair. Late one night I called and went to her apartment to try, one more time, to "talk some sense into her."

She welcomed me into her home. I talked. I cried. I begged her to think of their children. I begged her to reconsider. She sat in front of me like an ice sculpture.

Through tears I finally said, "Your marriage is dead, isn't it?"

With an icy stare she said simply, "Yes. It's dead. It's over."

I couldn't control my crying. I could hardly speak. Those words were the final nail in my heart. I literally felt myself falling to pieces.

With stoic stillness she said, "I'm sorry you are so upset, Mama. But nothing will fix our marriage. There is nothing you can say or do that will change that."

I hugged her and cried. I tried to pray with her, but couldn't speak for the tears. I cried as I walked out the door. I cried as I drove home. I curled up in my bed and cried. I lay on the floor of my office and cried as I prayed. When I reached the point that I had no more tears left in me I heard God's Spirit speak to my heart.

"This is brokenness, Jean. If you want me to heal your heart, if you want me to put you back together and make you whole, this is where we have to begin. First brokenness, then healing, then wholeness."

I lay on the floor still and quiet.

"There is nothing you can do to heal your daughter's marriage. Just as there is nothing you can do to heal yourself, to make yourself whole."

I sensed God's peace and quietness slowly trickling into my mind and heart. He was putting the shards back together. He was bringing wholeness out of the brokenness.

"What your daughter is doing may or may not be right. It may or may not be best. But it is *her* decision. Now you must decide to stand with her, or against her."

Face down on the carpet I decided to stand with my baby girl. To give her and her children whatever support, acceptance and love I could offer.

* * *

My daughter and her husband are now divorced. Both of them still face struggles. Their children are still hurting. God has asked me to take some extraordinary steps to demonstrate my love — His love — and commitment to my daughter. Steps that I can take only because of the healing of my own heart.

It is through brokenness that I've experienced in a minute way the pain and grief our Heavenly Father feels for His children and our decisions. This shattered heart has been pieced back together by God so that I might learn to love my daughter, my former son-in-law, my grandchildren and other people with some of the intensity that is the impetus of His love for me.

* * *

More than fifty years ago my grandmother died. One of the few possessions of hers that I have is a ceramic dish. It is ornate with gold edging and multi-colored leaves painted around it. I cherished it not because it was beautiful to my personal taste, but because it was hers. I displayed it in our home as a reminder of her and of my childhood.

When our boys were about nine or ten years old they were playing around in the living room (as little boys will do) and one of them bumped the shelf holding that dish. It crashed to the floor and broke into dozens of pieces.

I sat in the floor, gathered the pieces, and cried.

Late that night I sat at our dining table and glued every sliver back together. It was a labor of love.

Now I display that dish with new purpose. I can't use it. It won't hold liquid. And now it's too fragile to be handled. At first glance it looks whole, though, because one side of the dish managed to stay intact during the fall. But up close anyone can see the cracks, the glue lines, the scars of that accident.

I keep and display that scarred dish for two reasons. It still reminds me of my grandmother and childhood fun at her home. But now it also reminds me that God specializes in using broken vessels. He is an expert at gluing all the pieces back together. He is the expert at putting broken and scarred vessels on display for His glory and our good.

It's amazing to me when I consider that God prefers broken vessels. He knows we cannot be used by Him while we are whole and strong and full of ourselves. It is when we fall apart, when our lives are shattered, and when we allow Him to glue us back together that our lives can best display His beauty.

36

Commandeer Cheer

Sylvia Stewart

As a missionary's child, I was well acquainted with starting over — and that included making friends. I rarely had friends for longer than two years; either my friends' families went back to their homes countries or ours did.

When my family was on furlough, in addition to having to start over, I knew I was an outsider. I was the only one in my school who had lived in a leaf-walled hut with a grass-thatched roof. Nobody else in my school had seen pythons, lions, or Cape buffalo in the wild. Not one other student knew the misery of tropical diseases, nor the delight of speaking an African language as if it were their own. That set me apart and made me different — even peculiar — and being different and peculiar isn't appealing.

When I was eighteen, my parents returned to the mission field, leaving me alone, college-bound, in Washington state. My only sibling, a cherished brother, lived far away, and I had no other relatives nearby.

A doleful demeanor is never attractive, so I became acquainted with only a few people. However, I had a job, my own apartment, and the used car my parents had given me, so I had all I needed — except family and friends. For many days, I felt as blue as the vast ocean that separated me from all I held dear.

One morning, I caught a glimpse of my unhappy face in the mirror. "Cheer up!" I said to myself. "Surely, by now, you know that no one wants to make friends with a grumpy-puss." And to prove to myself that I could smile, I produced a cheesy grin for my mirror image. I laughed out loud at my silliness and the grotesque-though-comic smile. My spirits rose.

Conscripting cheerfulness may be a ploy we use on ourselves, but it can also be an act of faith. A cheerful smile reminded me that God brought goodness into my life, and that gave me a happier heart. Trusting God and acting as if I were happy brought about the happy heart I longed for. Deliberately discarding my lonely, gloomy face, and trading it in for a smiling one, made me happier and more friend-worthy.

In his excellent book, *A Touch of Wonder*, Arthur Gordon tells of a bleak period in his life during World War II. In 1942-1943, he was bivouacked in England's wet and muddy winter. Everyone he worked with was cold, homesick, and miserable except one sergeant, a crew chief, whose smiles, cheerfulness and good humor impressed him. One day, Lt. Gordon found this sergeant whistling as he worked in a freezing rain to get a skidded plane out of the mud and back on the runway. Lt. Gordon asked him how he could whistle and be so cheerful working in that mess. With a grin on his mud-spattered face, the sergeant said, "Lieutenant, when the facts won't budge, you have to bend your attitudes to fit them, that's all."

In the weeks ahead, I found that grasping cheerfulness and bending it to my will always worked. Seeing a smile in the mirror made me feel better. I often laughed out loud, even while berating myself for my foolishness. However, laughter lifted my spirits, even when I laughed alone.

It wasn't long before I had a bevy of new friends at my Christian college.

During a horrible start at sea, Paul admonished his shipmates to "bend their attitudes." "Be of good cheer," he said, even though their situation was grim.

Jesus also prompted his disciples, *"Be of good cheer; I have overcome the world,"* (John 16:33 KJV).

Acting as if I were happy, and trusting God to make it happen, brought me a cheerful heart and wonderful friends in the bargain. It's amazing what commandeering cheer will do to create the real attitude of acceptance, cheer and happiness.

37

Mona's Gift

Lydia E. Harris

Y ou should meet Mona," a friend told me. "Like you, she's crazy about tea."

When I phoned Mona (name changed) a few days later, we hit it off, and her bubbly laughter set me at ease. Although she was eager to explore tearooms together, I hesitated because of my full schedule; but she persuaded me.

Mona picked me up, and as we chatted, I learned she not only loved going out for tea, she dreamed of opening a French tearoom. She also possessed a wealth of tea knowledge and shared some of it over tea. Even though I enjoyed our teatime, I still wasn't sure I had time to invest in a new friendship.

Mona e-mailed ideas for more tea adventures, and gradually she worked her way into my life. Over several years, we visited one tearoom after another. As we lingered over tea, I learned about Mona's challenges raising two daughters as a single mom. As our relationship deepened, she began e-mailing me some of her prayer requests.

One day, as we sipped tea in a Scottish tearoom, the proprietors mentioned they had both had kidney transplants. Then Mona casually mentioned that she also had a kidney transplant. I was dumbfounded. She had never complained or mentioned her health challenges. Instead, she expressed trust in God and was full of joy and hope. But her transplant did explain her frequent hospitalizations between our tea jaunts.

One summer evening, instead of going out for tea, I invited Mona to stop by our home for tea and scones after work. I set the cart outside for tea *al fresco*. She was delayed, so I made more tidbits while I waited. By the time she arrived, I had prepared a full tea! Mona laughed when she saw all the goodies and savored every morsel. At dusk, we moved inside to keep chatting and sip more of her favorite Scottish tea blend. I sensed our hearts were blending too.

After she saw my tea collection, including the blue-and-white teapot from Romania, she said, "I just bought a picture at a garage sale that would look nice in your home." She went to her car and lugged back a large, beautifully framed painting of a blue-and-white teapot with background colors that matched my decor. As I leaned the painting against the wall, she explained, "I was late because I stopped by a friend's garage sale on the way here. My friend had saved this picture for me, certain I would love it."

"It's beautiful," I said, touching the walnut frame.

"I knew it didn't belong in my home," she said. "But I bought it because I thought God probably had someone else in mind." She smiled. "Now that I've seen your home I know it's you!"

I had admired similar expensive artwork in shops. Now, God had delivered the perfect picture right to my home. I felt like I had a personal shopper who knew what delighted me. I hung it in a prominent spot and often prayed for Mona when I looked at it.

Over the next year, Mona and I shared teatimes and recipes whenever we could. Then, I didn't hear from her for a long while. When I called to check on her, I learned that my tea friend had passed away. Conflicting emotions hit me. I felt sad and knew I would miss my tea buddy. But I also felt joy as I pictured her healthy and happy, serving tea parties in her heavenly French tearoom.

As I reflected on the loss of my friend and the memorable teatimes we had shared, I recognized what a precious gift God had blessed me with in Mona. I had given her a little of my time, but she gave me much more through her courageous example, cheerful heart, and warm friendship. I realized that when God brings someone unexpected into my life, He has a purpose beyond what I can see. And this time, part of His purpose was to bless me with a treasured friend.

Although our teatimes on earth have ended, I look forward to an eternity with Mona in heaven — worshipping our Lord and celebrating together.

38

The Light of Morning

Lola Di Giulio De Maci

My infant daughter quietly tiptoed into my life and then left as quickly as she came, seeing the light of only one morning. She arrived on a warm August evening and departed before the morning dew had a chance to settle on the pink roses outside my hospital window. Angela was nine hours and one minute old — but in my heart, she had lived a lifetime and a day.

"She's an angel," my mother said, trying to console me.

My best friend said, "Now she's with God."

"She's in a better place," they all said.

I know everyone tried their best to make me feel better, but none of those well-meant words worked for me. The mother in me wouldn't accept them. I didn't want an angel. And I didn't want her in a better place. I wanted her in my arms where she belonged.

Thus began a slow, uncharted journey down a long and painful path toward healing. Every morning I got out of bed and put one foot in front of the other, sometimes tripping over my own feet, sometimes slipping backward.

At times I walked the sights and sounds of shopping malls searching for a clue as to what had happened. Where did I think I would find the answer? In a bookstore? In a candle shop? In the children's section of a department store? Did I think someone would emerge from the shadows and slip me a piece of paper explaining why this had happened? No one ever approached me with an explanation; I never got that piece of paper. Walking helped anyway — and losing myself in the crowds.

Parks were good, too. I needed serenity and I went looking for it. I sat for hours on the soft, green grass and ran my fingers through patches of clover, looking for the good-luck one with four leaves.

Any little fragment of peace was welcomed. I would try to bottle up that feeling of tranquility and take it home with me, figuring I could keep it on a shelf somewhere for when I needed it.

My first-born daughter, Maria, was seven years old at this time and my son, Christopher, four. When the new school year began, Maria would enter third grade and Christopher would start kindergarten. I shuddered to think of being home alone without them.

On the first day of school, I took my son by the hand and walked into his kindergarten room with him.

"Can I help you?" I asked his teacher, noticing that she was trying to do ten things at once.

When she replied, "Yes!" without hesitation, I immediately took over the task of writing names on nametags.

I soon became a regular in the classroom — sharpening pencils, tying shoelaces, and setting up bulletin boards. I read stories to the students at story time and jumped headfirst into the book right along with the children. I loved being there. I had found a home.

It wasn't long before the principal approached me, offering me a new position. "I'd like you to teach fifth grade," she said, her nun's veil shadowing the look of horror on my face.

"Teach fifth grade?" I heard my voice echo. "I . . . I don't think so," I stammered. "I'm not ready." It would be a full-time assignment, and I wasn't sure I could take on such an enormous responsibility at that time in my life. I was petrified. I needed time to think.

I did a lot of soul searching in the next few months. I would see the principal coming toward me from across the playground, and I would hurry in the opposite direction. I didn't have an answer for her yet.

Finally, after much deliberation and prayer, I accepted the position of fifth grade teacher. My days were filled with lesson plans, classroom exercises, and recess duty. It wasn't long before I knew that I had made the right decision. I loved teaching. And I loved learning. I learned something new every day from my students who sat in front of me with questioning faces. I prayed daily that I had touched their lives as they had touched mine.

From time to time I would see a little girl skipping across the playground and suddenly remember a little girl who tugged at my soul one warm summer evening. My heart would skip a beat. Then I would realize how many children I had had the privilege of watching grow into beautiful, amazing adults since then. And my heart was full.

My once-seven-year-old daughter is now a teacher, and the kindergarten-aged son now a psychologist. I feel an overwhelming sense of pride when I see the good things they are doing with their lives.

Having now left my teaching days behind, I visit my daughter's classroom as a children's author, reading one of my stories to her kindergartners. On my way to Room 23, I pass clumps of clovers growing wild in patches of soft, green grass and realize how long it's been since I walked into my son's kindergarten room and read to his class at story time. I feel I've come full circle.

On the days I want to have lunch with my son, I have to travel several freeways to get to the Big City. When I arrive at the quaint, outdoor restaurant where we are to meet, I can hardly wait to see him. Sharing a vegetarian pizza, I see that he is happy — and that makes me happy.

Traveling home, I think of the baby who quietly tiptoed into my life . . . leaving as quickly as she came. "She's an angel who lives with God in a better place," they said. All those well-meant words have come to resonate somewhere in my soul, echoing their truth.

On the tenth anniversary of my baby's passing, I lay in bed sobbing — tears as fresh and raw as the night she was born. I cried because the pain of losing her still hurt . . . a lot. There are still tears now and then when I think of what might have been, but there is also much joy knowing that Angela is a part of my life and always will be. I am grateful to her for coming into my life and leading me down paths that might never have been.

As a teacher and writer, I have found solace and beauty in the many students who have graced me with their presence throughout the years. These children have been my greatest teachers. And I am honored to have been a part of their lives.

And as a mother . . . I have found solace and beauty in the joyful wonder of my children. They are truly my greatest gifts. I feel honored to share my life with them.

My blessings continue to arrive daily in the light of every new morning. I awaken to the miracle of a brand-new day, welcoming the surprises and possibilities life has to offer me.

And I am at peace.

39

Broken but Blessed

Kathy Pierson

On a hot day in July 1975, my husband, Gary, and I were twenty years old and had been married a little over a year. We stopped at my mom's house to pick up a blanket before we headed to the beach. With Gary behind the wheel of our 1964 Dodge, a gravel truck rumbled toward us in the other lane. An apartment complex being built on nearby property had caused construction traffic for weeks.

Without warning, the gravel truck made a right turn in front of us from the left lane.

Gary slammed on the brake and yanked the steering wheel to avoid a collision. When I saw the ten-wheeler looming before us I screamed and threw my hands in front of my eyes. We crashed into one of its large tires just behind the gas tank. Neither of us had our seatbelts on.

Everything seemed to happen in slow motion. As I flew forward, both arms hit the dashboard. My face then came up under the rearview mirror. The bare metal tore deep into my forehead and right upper lip. Propelled back again, my head landed against my husband's shoulder. Gary pulled off my bandana and held it on a large gash across my forehead.

I could hear sirens and commotion in and around our car, but I couldn't open my eyes due to the painful glass shards from the mirror. A voice said, "I'm a paramedic and I need to place this collar around your neck." Someone held my head, while Gary slid from the driver's seat. With choreographed precision, they lifted my legs, swiveled my body and pulled me onto the hard surface of a backboard. As they strapped me onto it, someone said, "Let's get her into the ambulance before we evaluate her injuries."

Gary rode in the back with me, and patiently answered my question, "Which car were we in?" several times on the way to the hospital. I heard the medic tell him, "She's in shock. That's why she can't remember details."

Upon arrival at the emergency room, the staff converged upon me. As they cut away my clothes, I moaned in pain. They draped a sheet over my body and whisked me away for x-rays. When no neck or spinal injuries were found, the uncomfortable backboard was removed.

Back in the ER a male technician flushed my eyes so I could open them. Because my glasses were smashed in the accident, everything was still a blur. But I felt more secure with the ability to see when people approached.

Members of both our families floated in and out of the room. Gary stayed with me whenever possible. My mom and sister came in, took one look at my bruised, swollen face and gasped. As my mother wiped tears from her eyes, she said, "I heard sirens a short time after you left but it never occurred to me they were for you."

Later, when mom briefly stepped out, I looked at my sister and said, "I've wondered what God would use to bring me back to Him." I began to cry.

With tears in her eyes, she said, "What do you mean by that?" She had no idea I led a double life and had been running hard from God. But as I lay, quite broken, I knew I had reached a turning point in my life. Four years earlier, in the summer of 1971, I'd given the Lord control of my life at a Christian camp. Since then I had made several wrong turns in my relationship with God. I'd rebelled against the Lord and made some poor choices. And now I lived a very hypocritical life. Although singing in the choir and teaching Sunday school I still chose to live in defiance of my Savior.

Before long, a fresh-out-of-college orthopedic surgeon arrived, clad in a bright Hawaiian shirt. I learned his wind-tossed hair was a result of his ride to the hospital in his convertible Jeep. His appearance didn't boost my confidence, but he proved to be an excellent doctor.

"You're one lucky young lady," he told me. "Your left arm is broken as well as your right wrist and ring finger, but you have no internal injuries."

I lay on the sterile white sheets and thanked God I had been spared anything more serious.

He ordered an over-the-elbow cast be applied to my left arm, and a shorter cast administered to the other. I was admitted to the hospital that evening. Before Gary left, he placed the call button for the nurse under my right hand. Later, when I tried to push it, I didn't have the strength.

I'd never felt so helpless and alone. I cried out to the Lord and confessed my sins. He immediately forgave me and embraced my wayward heart, but I suspected it would take some time before I could forgive myself.

The words of Psalm 51:1-2 expressed my heart so well: *Have mercy on me, O God, according to your unfailing love; according to your great compassion blot out my transgressions. Wash away all my iniquity and cleanse me from my sin.*

That night I surrendered to God's will for my life, and His peace and joy washed over me. The guilt and shame were gone, and I felt His presence with me. I knew, without a shadow of doubt, God had used this horrible accident to interrupt my downward spiritual course and bring me back into right relationship with Him.

A few days after the accident, my brother-in-law visited the facility where our car had been towed. As he gazed at the immense damage, a man came along-side him and said, "I bet no one survived that wreck." When David shared our story with him, the man was amazed.

A week after my eight-day hospital stay, over one hundred stitches were removed from my face. Small strips of sterile tape were applied for several weeks to keep the skin from pulling at the scars. Despite that, I didn't hide at home. I continued to go to church and run errands with Gary, as my energy would allow. Naturally, people were curious how I broke not one, but both of my arms. We told and retold our story to waitresses, store clerks, friends, and strangers. What a blessing to share how God had spared our lives.

Since our home didn't have air conditioning, managing with both arms in plaster casts was difficult. But it was a huge blessing to be able to bend my right arm in the weeks to follow.

My time of isolation was well spent. During the months of recovery, I wrote out and memorized two hundred and forty Bible verses.

Healing wasn't easy, physically or spiritually. I had to have an operation on my left arm where tendons had become entangled in the shattered bone. After a bone graft, surgeries to insert — and later remove — a four-inch steel plate, and months of physical therapy, I began to regain my strength. Spiritually, whenever I faced temptation, or felt myself slipping into self-condemnation and shame, I ran to God and trusted His promises.

Over forty years later, I'm a board certified biblical counselor. I lead women's Bible studies, and Gary and I are involved in ministry at prisons and children's homes. And all those verses memorized during my recovery? I return to them continually, to encourage myself as well as the people to whom we minister. God knew how valuable those scriptures would be to me now, just as He knew He would use this trial to refine me, so I would come forth as gold. The Lord never wastes any of our experiences.

When I counsel people who have traveled far from God, or have experienced trauma they think God can't use for good in their lives, I know what to tell them.

God is good, and faithful to save, even when it means saving us from ourselves.

40

The Longest Night

Robert B. Robeson, LTC, USA Ret.

More than twenty-nine years had elapsed since my 1969-1970 Vietnam combat tour of duty when I received a letter from Charles Harris. Charles, one of my former flight medics, had won two Silver Stars — America's third highest award for heroism — in less than a month and a half during that war.

Harris's letter provided new information and insight concerning a bizarre helicopter medical evacuation mission that could have claimed the lives of his crew, my crew, and ten wounded Americans at dawn on May 1, 1970 near the edge of Hiep Duc. Hiep Duc was a notoriously dangerous settlement approximately thirty-six miles southwest of our unit at Red Beach in Da Nang.

On April 30, 1970 I was unit commander of the 236th Medical Detachment (Helicopter Ambulance). At 2100 hours (9 P.M.), I was in Dust Off[1] flight operations at Red Beach when an urgent call was broadcast over our FM radio.

"Da Nang Dust Off, this is Charger Dust Off. Dust Off 6-0-8 was just shot down at Hiep Duc with 10 U.S. wounded aboard. Request another crew be sent to cover their AO (area of operations) until they can be evacuated. Also, be advised that there are at least two reported enemy .51-caliber machine guns working in that vicinity. Gunships are on station."

The longest night of my twenty-seven years on Earth had just begun.

An initial decision was easy for me to make. One of our six UH-1H

(Huey) helicopters with fourteen Americans aboard had been shot down. As unit commander, I wasn't about to ask others to do what I wasn't willing to do myself. So I asked for a volunteer crew to go with me to get them out.

For as long as I could remember, my father — a Protestant minister — had taught me to believe that God is my constant source of courage and strength. I'd learned as a small child that relying on Him for guidance and protection was never a sign of weakness. Now I had a premonition that a need for this "source" of power would be in great demand before the night was over.

This wasn't a new experience for me. In the previous nine months, I'd had seven of my helicopters shot up by enemy fire and had been shot down twice. I'd flown over nine hundred missions for more than 2,300 patients. In the previous thirty days, alone, our thirteen pilots and flight crews had had sixteen helicopters either shot up or shot down due to heavy action in our area of operation. We'd gone through our authorized inventory of six helicopters nearly three times.

Dust Off flying was a profession precariously balanced between joy and sorrow, pain and pleasure. It was intense and meaningful. As supposed noncombatant medical personnel, we pilots often talked among ourselves about the daily danger and death faced on nearly every mission. That was the nature of this beast called "war." Sometimes you were able to evade and outrun that bear. Sometimes the bear would lay in wait and attack you before you had time to react and attain safety for yourself and your patients.

Unit pilots referred to the Hiep Duc Valley, where Hiep Duc was located, as "Ulcer Alley" and "Death Valley" because it was a main North Vietnamese Army infiltration route. We had more aircraft shot up in this stretch of dangerous real estate than anywhere else in our 5,000-square-mile AO.

As we took off and flew over the U.S. Marine base on Freedom Hill, located toward the southern edge of Da Nang and adjacent to Da Nang

Air Force Base, I invoked my usual prayer for our safety and that of those we sought to evacuate.

Charger Dust Off, our field-site battalion aid station, was located at Landing Zone Hawk Hill, thirty-two miles south of Da Nang and nineteen miles northeast of Hiep Duc. We received an update on what had happened from Charger's RTO (radio-telephone operator).

"6-0-8 took a bunch of hits on takeoff, lost their engine and had to autorotate (descend on just the energy in their main rotor blades alone) from about one hundred feet. I don't know how they got it down in one piece with all that weight aboard."

"Are they in a secure area?" I asked.

"'Firebird' gunships (Huey helicopters also stationed at Hawk Hill) have been relaying information to me," Charger replied. "They somehow landed on a bunker without tipping over, are in an ARVN (South Vietnamese Army) outpost, and have taken over one of the ARVN FM field radios. They're up our primary frequency and are directing gunship fire because the compound is currently under ground attack. So give them a call when you get in range."

"Roger that," I replied. "In the meantime, we'll be taking all of their missions until we can get them out."

In the distance, we could see the intense firefight enveloping the northern outskirts of Hiep Duc. Tracers from helicopter mini-guns formed red streams of fire earthward while green enemy tracers arced skyward or ricocheted off the ground into the air. Some of the green tracers looked as big as basketballs as they stalked their aerial targets.

"Well, Bill, they weren't kidding when they reported that .51-cals were out there," I told my copilot, WO1 Bill Payne, over the intercom. He'd only been in-country a month and a half.

For a moment, I fought an urge to politely complain to God.

"Dust Off 6-0-8, this is 6-0-5. How do you read me?" I broadcast over our FM radio.

"Got you loud and clear," CW2 Tim Yost, the aircraft commander replied.

"Is everyone okay, what's the tactical situation, and what kind of an area do you have for me to land to?" I asked.

"Negative on the landing," Yost replied. "It's too hot to get us out at this time. We got hosed-down pretty good, but everyone's okay. Doc (SP4 Harris, their medic) says all of our patients should be able to make it to first light."

"I don't want to leave you there overnight," I said.

"You can't risk it," Yost replied forcefully. "We're taking mortars, small arms, and .51-cals down here and there's barbed wire and concertina wire all over the place. I'm not even sure there'll be enough room to land near our bird in the daylight," he added. "It's just too hot, and we can't get eighteen on your bird, anyway. I recommend that you come back at first light to give it a shot. The gunnies should be able to keep their heads down until then."

"Okay," I grudgingly agreed, "but if things quiet down, have the Firebirds relay a request for us at Hawk Hill. We'll be back there covering your area until we can get you out. Over."

"I'd wanted to get them out of there as soon as possible, even if we were forced to make two trips. It was often better to attempt an evacuation sooner than later. Now, if something happened to them, I'd feel even more responsible. But Yost knew the ground situation better than I did, and I had to rely on his judgment. For the first time, intense anxiety crept over me as I banked toward Hawk Hill and darkness closed around us.

At our underground Dust Off hootch and bunker at Hawk Hill, across from the aid station, the rest of my crew didn't seem worried. SP5 Tom Franks, medic, SP4 Walt Tominaga, crew chief, and Payne kidded around under the two bare 100-watt lightbulbs dangling on cords from the ceiling. They fashioned a bull's-eye on heavy timber beams that served as walls and had a knife-throwing contest using their survival knives. I think it was just a way to lessen their own anxiety, knowing that their friends were still in jeopardy at Hiep Duc.

Not long after this, the lights were turned off and they fell asleep on their cots. I lay fully awake on mine. I still wore my boots and flight suit and my mind was going over the Hiep Duc terrain and the approach I'd have to make early the next morning. Thinking about those waiting .51-caliber machine guns didn't make it any easier

A .51-cal is so big and bad enough there is little that can protect you if someone is firing one of these weapons in your direction. Its projectiles simple go through everything in sight.

In the blackness of that underground bunker, I wrestled with a premonition of imminent death unlike anything I'd experienced before. I prayed that we would be able to get all of them out alive and that I wouldn't make any stupid decisions or pilot errors. All of us experienced fear and apprehension nearly every day in combat, but this was different. It seemed to permeate my entire being. My final request was that this heavy burden of foreboding and anxiety would be lifted.

It is often in the dark hours of trouble, self-doubt, and fear that many take refuge in biblical teaching and guidance. I remembered Psalm 46:1 (NAS): *God is our refuge and strength, a very present help in trouble.* But I still felt extreme anxiety over my responsibility for the safety of that crew and their patients . . . and then insomnia set in.

Realizing that sleep was out of the question, I quietly got up, walked outside and climbed into our helicopter. I mentally went over my tactical plan to get into that confined outpost. At first light, we'd fly out to LZ Karen at 2,000 feet, parallel the Song Thu Bon River between Karen and LZ Siberia (both American artillery bases), then drop down on the deck low-level and come in over the rooftops of Hiep Duc into the landing zone.

Taking my flashlight, I performed a thorough preflight inspection, wondering if another mission would be called in to take my mind off what was going to happen in a few hours.

Around what some referred to as the Hour of the Wolf, the night became quiet. Outgoing artillery from the other side of the hill had ceased. Troops manning the bunkers spaced around the base had settled in for their continuous watch. That was the moment, usually between 0100-0200 hours, when you stare at the ceiling or sky, stone cold awake, listening to the throbbing of your own heart and wondering *What in the world have I gotten myself into now?* The rest of my crew didn't appear to have any illusions about their life expectancy. They obviously had faith in my ability to complete the mission because Tominaga had even "pulled rank" on another crew chief to go along in an attempt to rescue his friends. I appeared to be the one having difficulty dealing with my personal insecurities.

I stood on the medevac landing pad for awhile looking at the stars and scanning the floodlit bunker line stretching around the base that was surrounded by eerie-looking rice paddies. I also observed a number of Viet Cong POWs sleeping under a series of lights in a guarded enclosure behind the aid station.

Then I went inside the aid station to check on the downed crew's current status and talk with our night shift RTO. It still felt like the Empire State Building was propped on my chest. The long weary wait was working overtime on my mind.

About 0400 hours, I returned to our aircraft. I probably looked as wired as if I'd spent the night inside the guitar of a heavy-metal band. I sat quietly in my armored cockpit seat and prayed for peace in my spirit.

That's when I recalled the words of Psalm 91:5 (NAS): *You will not be afraid of the terror by night; or of the arrow that flies by day.*

After a few minutes, I took a deep breath, inhaled the night air, and felt myself slowly starting to relax. My tension began to subside. In that special moment, I felt a rare sensitivity to life.

The sun began to faintly smear the eastern sky red, orange, and yellow as it slowly poked its head above the South China Sea on the horizon. Past, present, and future were in the process of merging. It was time to get out of Dodge. My crew was rousted from bed and we were soon airborne.

It was our turn in the barrel, now.

Halfway to Hiep Duc, I made contact with 6-0-8 again. Everyone was fine and their patients had survived the night. Things had quieted down, the enemy had slunk away, and the gunships had gone home. Yost later noted that there were enemy bodies still slung over the perimeter wire but, because of the gunship cover, and their ability to communicate directly by radio to the pilots and direct their fire, the outpost had not been overrun.

As we talked, the pilot of another aircraft broke into our conversation. It was a Dust Off helicopter from Chu Lai, a unit farther southeast, bringing in a load of wounded to Hawk Hill. He'd monitored our conversation and asked if we needed assistance. The first of my prayers was answered before we even approached Hiep Duc. Now we wouldn't have to make two trips. Payne gave him the coordinates and told him there would be four of the least seriously wounded for them to evacuate.

The downed crew had already removed all three radios from their downed bird to keep them from falling into enemy hands, so I requested that Yost get his crew of four and six of the most seriously wounded ready for us. In an effort to reduce weight I hadn't topped-off our fuel at Hawk Hill so I figured we could take their crew, six patients, three radios, and our crew of four without bleeding off too much engine rpm on takeoff. The other helicopter would only be about 15 minutes behind, to evacuate the other ambulatory patients.

"Okay, 6-0-8, we're about a minute out," I broadcast. "Get ready to pop a smoke and have everyone available to move quickly if we take any fire."

"Good copy."

It was now 0500 hours and dawn was just beginning to touch the mountaintops around Hiep Duc. I banked right around LZ Karen at 2,000 feet and pointed the nose of our bird toward the Vietnamese settlement, as we paralleled the river on our left. That was the moment when we all heard the distinctive belch of AK-47 rifle fire. In the early morning light, Payne and I witnessed something I'd never seen before in nearly nine hundred combat missions. I believe God allowed it to happen as a graphic reminder to me of His protecting grace and power. In the rising sun's rays we could actually *see* the enemy's non-tracer rounds' silvery reflections slicing through the air in front of our aircraft.

I immediately banked hard right into a tight spiral and dove for the deck. Then I keyed my mike. "Go ahead and pop smoke, 6-0-8. Be advised we're taking fire from across the river at the base of Siberia, so don't expose yourselves until we're down."

"Smoke's out."

"Got your purple smoke at our twelve o'clock," Payne said.

"Good color. That's us."

"Keep your heads down," I added. "Here we come."

I tore along dragging our skids a few feet above the sheet-metal rooftops of Hiep Duc. If these Vietnamese civilians weren't awake before, our eleven hundred horses pounding overhead probably did the trick.

As we bore down on the purple smoke at one hundred twenty knots, Yost scrambled out of a trench — raising his arms like Moses must have done prior to parting the Red Sea — and served as a ground guide. I side-slipped the aircraft, performed a hairy flare to reduce our airspeed and then skidded to a high hover above a tiny enclosure jammed with concertina wire.

I could see a huge smile spread across Yost's mustached face.

As soon as our skids touched down, tail rotor dangerously close to the heavily-coiled concertina wire, a bevy of shouts rang out as his crew charged out of their trenches.

They assisted six wounded comrades into our aircraft. PFC Gary Hagen, their crew chief, tossed the radios aboard as they packed themselves into every available niche and cranny of the cargo compartment. Then laughing and slapping us on our backs, they yelled above our Lycoming jet engine's roar, "Go! Go! Go!"

I'd had a host of athletic thrills in high school, college, and the military, but I'd never experienced the excitement and emotion of anything that compared to that moment. Using my collective control to pull in all of the available power our engine had, I hovered up until we were clear of the wire, then eased the nose over to gain translational lift and hunkered off toward the relative safety of LZ Karen to the southeast. I climbed to 2,000 feet while circling Karen in case we needed a safe landing area in an emergency. While we flew toward Hawk Hill, Payne briefed the Chu Lai crew who followed us in to evacuate the remaining four Americans.

We unloaded our wounded at the aid station pad, shut down the aircraft next to our bunker, and then walked with their weary crew to our mess hall. I spoke to each of them briefly before coming to Harris. He'd just been promoted to specialist four on February 17, 1970 and had only been in-country approximately three months. He was a short, soft-spoken, twenty-year-old from Falkland, North Carolina. His white T-shirt was covered with dirt and blood from treating his patients all night in a slit trench under fire. He'd helped to keep the lights lit in their lives throughout that chaotic and dangerous night in the dark.

"Chuck," I said, "I'm really proud of the job you did out there last night . . . taking care of those guys."

He looked up, grinned self-consciously, and replied, "Sir, I wasn't worried at all. I knew you'd get us out."

I suddenly felt very old and disgusted with myself. Here was a gutsy young medic who'd had complete faith in our ability to get to them. Yet I'd spent that interminable night primarily preoccupied with my own anxieties about how I was going to extract them, rather than on how I believed God would help me to make the right decisions and prepare the way for us. This young medic's faith in me made my faith in God look suspect as my thoughts had wavered on the proper course of action to take. It was a humbling and illuminating experience.

War is dirty and ugly. It is killing and maiming, suffering and hardship. Yet, in a perverse sort of way, it is also the springboard for acts of human courage, self-sacrifice, and nobility of spirit. The crew of 6-0-8 demonstrated all of that and more. They'd tried to lighten the dark moments of the night with comradely caring of the sort that helps soldiers survive wounds, shot up aircraft, and enemy action. And they all proved to me that love and determination can be forces stronger than chaotic and dangerous circumstances.

If we hadn't gone through that testing time, I would have missed an opportunity to see what God could do with bad news.

It became apparent to me, once again, that if you never go, you never get. Obstacles are mere hurdles to be leaped. Setbacks are opportunities to learn.

I believe when we descended into that treacherous valley for our fellow crew members and their patients, God was with us, pushing back my anxieties.

It embarrasses me now to recall my trial of faith and the initial fear I experienced during those missions, after all I'd previously been through. Over forty-seven years later, it's a fact and lesson I've never forgotten. I'm sure I never will.

Harris's letter provided additional background information I hadn't been aware of and ended with a memory that still appeared vivid to him over twenty-nine years later.

"I can remember thinking how beautiful the red cross on (the nose of) that chopper was when it popped-up over the crest of that hill the next morning," Harris wrote. "You were the one who came in and got us."

Coincidentally, on May 25, 2000, my wife received an e-mail from Gary Hagen.

It said, "Tell your husband 'hello' for me . . . I was the crew chief on that crew that he came in and picked up that morning after we were shot down in Hiep Duc on May 1, 1970. Tell him 'thanks' again for me."

Yost, WO1 Ed De La Vergne (copilot), Harris, and Hagen all were awarded Silver Stars for that night's action. And these two enlisted men were thanking *me*? That's the kind of true American heroes I was surrounded by in combat.

Postscript

The downed helicopter at Hiep Duc was so riddled with hundreds of additional bullet holes, from being exposed to that night-long firefight that my superiors gave me authorization to call in a U.S. Air Force jet to blow it in place so it wouldn't fall into enemy hands.

[1]"Dust Off" was the radio call sign used by U.S. Army Medical Service Corps evacuation crews who flew unarmed helicopters to evacuate wounded and dead civilians and soldiers on both sides of the action. Some people believe this term came from the dust our helicopters kicked up when we were landing. It is actually an acronym for dedicated, unhesitating service to our fighting forces.

41

River of Life

Bob Blundell

Along the muddied banks of the Jordan, thin reeds the color of sage reached toward the sky, bending gently in the breeze. A silver mist clung to the water's surface, and as the sun pierced the clouds, the haze glistened in the morning light. I would have preferred solitude, being alone with my thoughts and reflections. But other travelers stood along the water's edge this morning. They had come, like me, to pay homage to this sacred place, and all that had transpired here.

There was a surreal sense of calm and tranquility in the air. And human voices had faded to muffled whispers, as if to acknowledge the respect and silence that the river demanded. The only other sounds were those created by God Himself: the fluttering murmurs of the birds in the trees, and the gurgling melody of the water as it made its journey to the sea.

I leaned against the cold steel of the railing, a modern-day boundary built along the river's edge. The bright blue paint that covered it symbolized a contrast of the new versus the old. A reflection of our world today versus our beginning. I watched the flow run steadily past me, carrying leaves from the palms that dotted the banks. And there were deep furrows etched along the surface, like scars on an ancient warrior.

It was narrower than I had imagined, hardly twenty yards at its widest point. And the eddying stream was the color of burnt jade, dark and murky. The ripples spun and turned along their path, and as I reflected on all that the Jordan had witnessed over the centuries, I was suddenly struck by my own frailty and insignificance.

I closed my eyes and tried to imagine what it must have been like. As the warmth of the sunlight touched my cheeks, I began to see it unfold before me.

* * *

To the south, in the shallowest part of the river, stood a man. He had appeared one day "walking out of the desert wearing clothing of camel hair and a leather belt." His name was John. He was gaunt, with hair the color of wood smoke, and a beard tangled and twisted as a fisherman's net. His face was dark as tarnished bronze and chiseled with wrinkled lines of age. Even from a distance his deep-set eyes gleamed in the sunlight.

On the shore behind him, a small fire burned steadily, sending wisps of blue smoke curling into the air. Huddled near the flames, seeking shelter from the morning chill, sat two of his followers. These men had left the lives they had known, committing themselves to his teachings, and to the God he had been sent to prepare the way for.

Through the slate-colored mist I could see a second figure suddenly emerge from the opposite bank. He was tall, clad in a simple alabaster-colored robe that hung to his sandaled feet. Hair, the color of cinnamon, fell to his shoulders and I could see his mahogany eyes shining brightly in the sunlight like a candle flickering in a gentle breeze. I knew instantly who He was, and I felt my heart race. I watched Him as He stepped into the river and made His way across to the other side where the John stood. Waiting.

When they came together, He gently caressed John's face, like a father's loving touch of his only son. Then they waded toward the middle until dark streams of water swirled around their waists. I watched as John baptized Him, just as he had done to so many others before Him.

As our Savior's head emerged from beneath the surface of the water, a dazzling beam of light cascaded through the clouds "like a dove" sailing toward the earth. And a thunderous voice came down from the heavens shaking the ground around me, "This is my Son in whom I am well pleased."

Wind gusted across the surface of the Jordan, churning a pale blue mist into the air, before disappearing, as if it were sucked into the clouds. And as quickly as it had departed, calm once again settled over the ancient river.

* * *

Slowly the images in my mind began to fade. My eyes fluttered open and I squinted into the morning sunlight that filtered through the trees. There was a sweet smell in the air, like that of honeysuckle, and I took a deep calming breath, awestruck by the moment. I knew I would never be able to fathom what it would have been like that day. Had I been standing there in the shallows when the Holy Spirit spilled down from heaven, the beauty would have been like none ever seen by human eyes.

I knew this moment along the Jordan would remain with me for as long as I lived. It would always be a reminder of the power and glory of God. And I was overwhelmed with gratitude that He had blessed me with the opportunity to be a witness to one of His greatest creations.

Below me, the dark water flowed tirelessly. Always moving. Relentless in its journey.

This river has seen many extraordinary miracles over the centuries. Sins has been washed away. New lives have been formed. Like so many of us in our modern world, there would have been people who had lost their way. People who stepped into the water, broken and full of despair, only to emerge with joy and peace in their hearts.

Be still and know that I am God
Psalm 46:10

About the Authors

Nancy Kelley Alvarez loves to share stories that inspire risk-taking faith and courage, making a positive difference in the world one person at a time through the love of Jesus Christ. She is especially passionate about helping oppressed women survive and thrive in today's challenging world. She is the author of two novels, *The Butterfly Impact* and *The Opportunity*. She lives in the Philippines with her Filipino husband, Al, on the island of Iloilo. Together they train others how to tell short Bible stories in their own language. Following Jesus is a joyful but challenging adventure she wouldn't trade for anything. You can connect with her on Facebook or at pnalvarez@yahoo.com.

Bob Blundell is a former mid-level manager who spent his career in the oil industry. Since retiring, he has rekindled his passion for writing. He has had previous work published in magazines such as *Testimony, Liguorian, The Living Pulpit, Spectrum, Reachout Columbia,* and *Torrid Literary Review*. He has also been a contributor to other *Divine Moments* collections. Bob and his wife Dee live in the Houston area.

Krista Lynn Campbell is a freelance writer and an advocate for children living in poverty. Writing to sponsored children around the world and packing shoeboxes for Operation Christmas Child keeps her busy throughout the year. She lives in Pennsylvania with her husband, Jay.

Ken Carver, freelance journalist, writer, and editor in Collierville, Tennessee, has written feature articles, personality profiles, and devotions for LifeWay publications, plus newspaper features for Memphis' *The Commercial Appeal*, Collierville's *The Collierville Herald* amon others. He is a member of Byhalia Christian Writers, Editorial Freelancers Association and is a board member of the Mid-South Christian Writers Conference. Carver and his wife Lynn have two sons and one grandson and are active members of Collierville First Baptist Church.

Steve Carter has lived exclusively in the South. A Bible College graduate, he has spent the majority of his life in service to The Risen Christ. Currently, his primary ministry is safeguarding congregations by training and participating in armed security teams. A physical fitness enthusiast, he has participated in numerous running and bicycling sports, with the most noteworthy being peddling across the Continental United States twice. He spends his leisure time enjoying his grandchildren and playing drums.

Diana Derringer is an award-winning writer and author of *Beyond Bethlehem and Calvary: 12 Dramas for Christmas, Easter, and More!* Hundreds of her articles, devotions, dramas, planning guides, Bible studies, and poems appear in 40-plus publications, including *The Upper Room, The Secret Place, Clubhouse, Kentucky Monthly, Country,* and *Missions Mosaic,* plus several anthologies. She also writes radio drama for Christ to the World Ministries. Her adventures as a social worker, adjunct professor, youth Sunday school teacher, and friendship family for international university students supply a constant flow of writing ideas. Visit her at dianaderringer.com. You can also find her on Facebook, Twitter, LinkedIn, Instagram, Goodreads, and Pinterest.

Lola Di Giulio Di Maci is a retired teacher with a Master of Arts in education and English. Her stories have appeared in numerous editions of *Chicken Soup for the Soul;* in the *Los Angeles Times* as a children's author; and in the *San Bernardino Sun, Fontana Herald News,* and *Inland Valley Daily Bulletin* as a columnist. When she writes, Lola knows she is doing what God meant for her to do. The mother of two daughters and a son, Lola writes overlooking the San Bernardino Mountains.

Tanja Dufrene has been married to her south Louisiana beau for 37 years. Having overcome many broken moments through the power of God's Word and the leading of His Spirit, she is passionate about helping others overcome as well. She writes a daily minute devotion posted to her Warrior of the Word Facebook page. You can learn more and connect with her at WarrioroftheWord.faith or follow her on Instagram, Twitter, and Pinterest as Warrior of the Word.

Ashley Dutch is 37 years old and lives in Crossville, Tennessee with her husband of two years. Her husband owns a pressure cleaning business and she is pursuing a ministry in Christian writing. They love to be out in God's creation, whether hiking in the woods or searching for seashells on the beach. The Lord is their true passion and they enjoy spending their time serving Him.

Joanna Eccles founded wordsfromthehoneycomb.com to encourage people to grow in Christ. She desires to shape culture by addressing truths in relatable ways. She has led Bible studies for over 15 years and completed the year-long C. S. Lewis Fellows Program. She is passionate about discipleship and helping people know God better. Joanna enjoys coffee and reading. She lives in Virginia.

Terri Elders, LCSW, a lifelong writer and editor, has contributed to over 100 anthologies, including multiple editions of *Chicken Soup for the Soul*. After a quarter-century odyssey, include a decade overseas with Peace Corps, she returned to her native California. She's happy to be back near her son, old friends, and her beloved Pacific Ocean. She blogs at http://atouchoftarragon.blogspot.com.

Peggy Ellis has been a freelance editor for 48 years, and an author for considerably less. Over the past 25 plus years, she has published regularly in such magazines as *Good Old Days, Reminisce, Rock and Gem, Aquarium, True Story, Splickety, Woman's World,* and *Righter Monthly Review,* now the *RPG Digest,* the latter in print and ezine. She has compiled and edited three anthologies for her writers' group: *Challenges on the Home Front World War II* (Chapel Hill Press, 2004), *Lest the Colors Fade* (Righter Books, 2008), and *A Beautiful Life and Other Stories* (Righter Books, 2010). Each contains her short fiction, memoirs, and research. She is a contributing author to books in Grace Publishing's *Divine Moments* Series, and the second edition of *Challenges on the Home Front, World War II.* You may contact Peggy at peggyellis.com — book editor, LinkedIn Peggy Lovelace Ellis, and Good Reads.

Diana Flegal lives in Asheville, North Carolina. A Bible College major in Missions and Anthropology, Diana has been a medical missionary to Haiti, a women's speaker, and Bible study leader. One of her life's highlights has been teaching apologetics to high school students.

Jean Matthew Hall lives in LaGrange, Kentucky. Her stories and articles appear in a variety of inspirational magazines and anthologies including *The Embrace of a Father, Whispering in God's Ear, Chicken Soup for the Chocolate Lover's Soul, The Ultimate Gardener, God Makes Lemonade, Christmas Miracles, The Spirit of Christmas* and *Additional Christmas Moments.* Jean's first children's picture book, *God's Blessings of*

Fall, was released in 2019. It is available from any online book dealer. You can read more from Jean at jeanmatthewhall.com/blog or at Jean Matthew Hall Author on Facebook.

Lydia E. Harris has been married to her college sweetheart, Milt, for more than 50 years. She enjoys spending time with her family, which includes two married children and five grandchildren aged 10 to 21. She is the author of two books for grandparents: *Preparing My Heart for Grandparenting: for Grandparents at Any Stage of the Journey* and *In the Kitchen with Grandma: Stirring Up Tasty Memories Together*. With a master's degree in Home Economics, Lydia creates and tests recipes with her grandchildren for Focus on the Family children's magazines. She also pens the column "A Cup of Tea with Lydia," which is published in the US and Canada. It's no wonder she is known as Grandma Tea.

Helen L. Hoover and her husband are retired and live in the Ozark Mountains of southern Missouri. Sewing, reading, and knitting are her favorite pastimes. However, caring for the flower and vegetable gardens and helping her husband with home projects receive priority on her time. Visits with their children, grandchildren and great-grandchildren are treasured. She is thrilled to be included in 27 compilation books. *Word Aflame Publishing, The Secret Place, Word Action Publication, The Quiet Hour, LIVE, The Lutheran Digest, Light and Life Communications, Chicken Soup for the Soul,* and *Victory in Grace* have published her devotionals and personal articles.

Alice Klies has written since she could hold a pencil. She is president of Northern Arizona Word Weavers. Through their encouragement Alice began to submit her work for publication. She has nonfiction and fiction stories published in 25 anthologies. She is an eleven-time contributor to *Chicken Soup for the Soul* books and has articles in *Angels on Earth, AARP* and *Wordsmith Journal*. She has been featured in the *Women of Distinction* magazine. Little Cab Press released *Pebbles in My Way*, a fiction based on her testimony, in September 2017. In addition to her involvement in Word Weavers, she is a Stephens Minister in her church. Alice serves on two non-profit boards: The Verde Valley Humane Society and Sisterhood Connections LTD. Alice is a retired teacher who resides with her husband and two Golden Retrievers in Cottonwood,

Arizona. She prays her stories cause a reader to smile, laugh, or cry, and most of all turn their eyes to God who loves them.

Rita Klundt began her second career as an author, speaker, and story collector after nearly 30 years of nursing. Her first book, *Goliath's Mountain*, tells a poignant and tragic love story that gives readers a view into the heart of a family touched by mental illness and suicide. Rita's passion for true and transparent stories led her to write a second book and then encourage 26 of her friends to share their stories for a third — both scheduled for publication in 2021. She and her husband live in central Illinois and enjoy travel. They are excited about where this stage of life is taking them. Follow Rita and watch for more great stories at ritaklundt.com.

Kathleen Kohler writes for Christian and general market magazines, such as *Discipleship Journal, Focus on the Family, The Upper Room*, and *School Bus Fleet*, among numerous other publications. Since 2010 she's contributed to 23 anthologies, including 14 *Chicken Soup for the Soul* books, as well as books by Dr. Gary Chapman, and bestselling author, Cecil Murphey. She and her husband live in the Pacific Northwest, and have three children and seven grandchildren. Visit kathleenkohler.com to read more of her articles about the ups and downs of life.

Diana Leagh Matthews is a vocalist, speaker, writer, and genealogist. During the day, she is a certified Activities Director for a nursing facility. She is a Christian Communicators graduate. She has been published in several anthologies, including the *Divine Moments* series. She currently resides in South Carolina. Visit her at DianaLeaghMatthews.com and alookthrutime.com.

Norma C. Mezoe has been a published writer for 35 years. Her writing has appeared in books, devotionals, take-home papers and magazines. She is active in her church in a variety of roles. Norma became a Christian at the age of 15, but didn't grow spiritually in a significant way until a crisis at the age of 33 brought her into a closer relationship with the Lord. Norma may be contacted at normacm@tds.net.

Lynn Mosher has had her socked feet firmly planted in the Midwest since she drew her first breath. She has lived with her hubby since 1966 in their family nest, emptied now of three chicklets and embracing two giggly granchicklets. Although an upheaval of illness has stalked her for many years, her deepest passion is sharing her devotions, inspirational stories, and graphics on social media, fulfilling God's call on her life to encourage others and glorify the Lord with her writing.

Dr. Jayce O'Neal is the pastor of RED Church in Virginia Beach. RED Church is a growing church community focused on seeing people discover redemption through Jesus. Dr. Jayce is also the author of *One-Minute Devotions for Boys, No Girls Allowed: Devotions for Boys, Crazy Circus World* and *100 Answers to 100 Questions Every Graduate Should Know.* He is an instructor at Regent University and is an avid sports fan who enjoys cheering for his favorite sports teams while eating pizza with a fork. He has a Doctorate, two Masters Degrees, a Bachelor of Science, and a small trophy for perfect attendance in Sunday school from when he was nine. He currently resides with his fantabulous wife and four children in the Virginia Beach area. For more information about Dr. Jayce visit Drjayce.com.

Cheryl A. Paden is an inspirational, devotional, and memoir writer, and speaker. She has been published in magazines, anthologies, and devotional books. She created and published a combination planner/prayer journal titled *Sacred Balance: Discovering Sacred Balance in an Out-of-Balance World.* Cheryl has worked as a registered nurse, in apartment management, and bookkeeping, and as a local pastor in the United Methodist Church. She is a member of the Nebraska Writers Guild, The Jerry Jenkins Writers Guild, Compel/Proverbs 31, and My Thoughts Exactly (a local writers group). She teaches Writing from Life at the local community college. In her spare time she enjoys knitting, quilting, and reading and writing memoir. She and her husband of over 40 years have three sons and seven perfect grandchildren. They live in Fremont, Nebraska.

Kathy Pierson is a retired EMT and a member of the Blue Ridge Writers Group. Her stories have been published several times in *Power for Living, Now What?* In addition, she has written articles for her local newspaper. One of her stories took first place in a Silverarts competition. Kathy and her husband are privileged to reside in

Hendersonville, North Carolina near their two children and three grandchildren.

Barbie Porter is a Christ-follower who cherishes her family and friends, lives to serve others, and enjoys sharing heart-to-heart conversations over a cuppa. She and her husband, Ralph, are missionaries to Haiti, the Appalachian Mountains, and love placing Bibles through the Gideons International. They call Kentucky home and are the proud parents of seven children, 17 grandchildren and six great-grandchildren.

Patricia Dokter Ritsema is a life-long educator who has taught in preschool, university, and everything in between. She specializes in Christian education and special education, and from her experiences as a teacher, principal, and counselor she has gathered a lifetime of valuable knowledge. After she and her husband retired, her husband was diagnosed with pancreatic cancer. From those excruciating moments she began to write through her avalanche of emotions, their remaining months together, and her grief upon his death. Having developed a love for writing from those painful experiences, she is now completing her very first book for parents of children with learning disabilities and ADHD, intending to provide her readers with the same hope the Lord has given her.

Robert B. Robeson has been published 930 times in 330 publications in 130 countries. This includes the *Reader's Digest, Positive Living, Soldier of Fortune, Logbook, Writer's Digest, Frontier Airline Magazine, Chicken Soup for the Soul, War Cry* and *Newsday*, among others. He's also been featured in 65 anthologies. He retired from the U.S. Army as a lieutenant colonel, upon completing a 27½-year career on three continents and in combat in Vietnam (1969-1970). Nineteen of those years were spent as a helicopter medical evacuation pilot. After his military retirement, he was a newspaper managing editor and columnist. He has a BA in English from the University of Maryland, College Park, and has completed extensive undergraduate and graduate work in journalism at the University of Nebraska, Lincoln, and is also a professional (life) member of the National Writers Association, VFW, Dustoff Association, and the Distinguished Flying Cross Society. Robeson has won four international Amy Writing Awards and 15

Freedoms Foundation at Valley Forge George Washington Honor Medals for articles and speeches on freedom. He's also won or placed in over 150 international and national writing contests. He lives in Lincoln, Nebraska with Phyllis, his wife of 52 years.

Christina Sinisi, a member of the American Christian Fiction Writers, writes stories about families, both the broken and blessed. Her works include a semi-finalist in the Amazon Breakthrough Novel Award Contest and the American Title IV Contest in which she appeared in the top ten in the *Romantic Times* magazine. Her published books include *The Christmas Confusion* and the upcoming *Sweet Summer*, the first two books in the Summer Creek Series, as well as *Christmas on Ocracoke*. By day, she is a psychology professor and lives in the Lowcountry of South Carolina with her husband and two children and cat Chessie Mae. She can be found at Christina Sinisi-Author on Facebook and ChristinaSinisi.com.

Sylvia Stewart was a missionary kid to the Belgian Congo. After she married, she and her husband spent 21 years as missionaries in Malawi, Africa, and 11 years in Ethiopia, working mostly doing Bible College ministry. Now retired with four grown children, eleven grandchildren, and three great-grandchildren, she writes short Christian fiction, articles for her denomination's magazines, and Sunday school papers.

Nate Stevens, a lifelong student of Scripture, has also enjoyed a banking career in a variety of leadership roles. He is the author of *Matched 4 Life, Deck Time with Jesus, Transformed: Until Christ Is Formed in You,* and *Conformed: Into the Likeness of Christ* as well as a contributing author in several of the books in the *Divine Moments* series. He writes online articles for ChristianDevotions.us and KingdomWinds.com as well as several other ministries. Additionally, he co-founded and leads Fusion, a Christian singles ministry. A popular speaker and teacher at conferences, seminars, and Bible study groups, he speaks on a wide variety of topics. Nate has two adult children. He and his wife, Karen, live near Charlotte, North Carolina. Follow Nate and find more resources at natestevens.net.

Nanette Thorsen-Snipes, mother of four and grandmother of eight, has contributed stories to more than 60 compilation books. She loves to spend a weekend in the mountains at a bed-and-breakfast and explore the countryside, especially waterfalls. She has authored one Arch book for children, *Elijah Helps the Widow*, many stories and reprints in Christian magazines, stories and photos for *Georgia Magazine*, and columns for weekly newspapers. A professional editor since 2004, she specializes in children's fiction, nonfiction, and memoirs.

Annmarie Tait resides in Conshohocken, Pennsylvania with her husband, Joe Beck. Annmarie's stories appear in many volumes of *Chicken Soup for the Soul*, and Grace Publishing's *Divine Moments* series. In addition to writing, she enjoys baking, and crochet, along with singing and recording American and Irish folk songs with her husband Joe. Contact Annmarie at irishbloom@aol.com.

Denise Valuk lives and writes from San Antonio, Texas. She is a *Guideposts Magazine* Writer's Worship Winner from 2012 and has been published in *Guideposts* and *Mysterious Ways* magazines. She has also previously been published the *Divine Moments* series and in several *Chicken Soup for the Soul* publications. She currently serves on the board of Junior Wildlife Ranger, a non-profit organization that creates educational programs for children to learn at national wildlife refuges. Denise is honored to have created the educational content for Balcones Canyonlands National Wildlife Refuge in Texas. She may be reached at denisemarievaluk@gmail.com or her website, denisevaluk.com.

Beverly Varnado is an award-winning author and screenwriter as well as a blogger and artist. She has a Christmas novella from Anaiah Press, *A Season for Everything*, a sequel to her novels *A Plan for Everything* and *The Key to Everything* — all set in the fictional town of Worthville, Georgia. Her blog, *One Ringing Bell*, has nearly 1,000 posts in its archives. Her work has been featured on World Radio, in *The Upper Room Magazine*, and in several other periodicals, anthologies, and online sites. She has been a finalist for the prestigious Kairos Prize in screenwriting and also has several other non-fiction and fiction books available. Having recently exhibited in a state university gallery, she is always working on a new painting. She lives in north Georgia with her husband, Jerry, and is Mom to three and Mimi to two. Learn more at Beverly Varnado. com.

Yvonne Lehman
1936-2021

Yvonne Lehman, award-winning, best-selling author of 73 books, including 57 novels, and more than 3,000,000 books in print, has been published throughout the US and in Germany, Holland, and Norway. Her genres include Romance, Women's Fiction, Christian Fiction, Cozy Mystery, Young Adult, Biblical times and stories including suspense, humor, true events and thought-provoking plots with intriguing characters.

Yvonne founded and for 25 years directed the Blue Ridge Mountains Christian Writers Conference, held at the Ridgecrest North Carolina Conference Center. After turning that conference over to another leader, she founded and directed the Blue Ridge Autumn in the Mountains Novelist Retreat for 12 years.

From 2015-2021 Yvonne compiled and edited the *Divine Moments* anthologies published by Grace Publishing House. Two books in the series were Selah Awards finalists: *Moments with Billy Graham* in 2019 and *Christmas Stories* in 2021.

Some of Yvonne's personal awards and honors include

- The Award of Excellence in Christian Literature presented by the Billy Graham School of Christian Writing – for the best work submitted by a former year's student at their conference in Minneapolis, Minnesota.
- National Reader's Choice Award for *Mountain Man*
- Romance Writers of America's Booksellers Best Award for *The Stranger's Kiss* (Heartsong)
- #6 CBA Best-Seller List (over 100,000 sold) – Crossings hardcover – *A La Mode* (*Summer Dreams* collection)
- #15 CBA Best-Seller List – *Dear Jane*
- #15 CBA Best-Seller List – *Carolina* – reprinted as *Finding Love in the Blue Ridge Mountains*

9 781604 950755